"Melissa and Sissy are women I respect as authors, counselors, and mentors to countless girls across the country including my own daughters. I can't wait for them to be old enough to read this book. I am grateful to have these insightful women helping all of our girls find their way through the haze of adolescence into the girls God has made them to be.
Sigmund Brouwer, Author Broken Angel: A Novel, Father of 2

"I'll be honest, I would rather watch grass grow than read a book, but Mirrors and Maps surprisingly changed all of that! From the very first page, I was wrapped up, hanging on each word written so eloquently and genuinely by Sissy and Melissa. I was captivated by the sheer humor and authenticity of this easy-to-read brilliant piece of work. My only regret is that I didn't have this useful resource when I was a young girl transitioning into teen-dom. It would've kept me out of trouble and made my parents life a lot easier! Thanks to the authors' empathetic, experienced hearts, girls everywhere – including me, a 26 year old – have a clearer understanding of how essential it is to
BE OURSELVES!
Lindsey Kane, Worship Leader & Recording Artist

youth
specialties

Mirrors and Maps:A Girl's Guide to Becoming a Teen
Copyright 2008 by Melissa Trevathan and Sissy Goff

Youth Specialties products, 300 S. Pierce St., El Cajon, CA 92020 are published by
Zondervan, 5300 Patterson Ave. SE, Grand Rapids, MI 49530.

ISBN 978-0-310-27918-1

Cover design by SharpSeven Design
Interior design by Brandi K. Etheredge

Printed in the United States of America

08 09 10 11 12 • 18 17 16 15 14 13 12 11 10 9 8 7 6 5 4 3 2 1

MIRRORS & MAPS

by
Melissa Trevathan and Sissy Goff

*This book is dedicated to all the Daystar girls and
Facebook friends who shared their wisdom with us for this
book: Allie, Anne Mason, Bethany, Betsy, Brenna, Brittany,
Caitlin, Callie, Campbell, Caroline, Cate, Catherine, Colleen,
Emilie, Emily, Elizabeth, Evie, Georgia, Grace, Hannah,
Hope, Jessi, Juliana, Julie, Kathleen, Kylie, Mackenzie,
Mamie, Marion, Marnie Kate, Mary, Mary Dea, Megan,
Meredith, Molly, Ouida, Rachel, Ruth, Sara, and Sarah.*

*And to the guys who graciously gave us their words:
Carter, Chris, David, Graham, Jake, Jamie, Jeff, Jordan,
Kendrick, Nathan, Nathaniel, Noah, and Taylor.*

We are grateful to have you as guides.

TaBLe OF CONTeNTS

Anne Lamott says that her best prayers are "Help me, help me, help me" and "Thank you, thank you, thank you." We have prayed both of them often in the writing of these two books. And we have spoken them (probably not often enough) to a group of people who have helpedlighten our loads during our chaotic counseling/book writing/summer camp directing kind of schedule. From a publishing standpoint, we are grateful for the wisdom of Sandy VanderZicht, Bob Hudson, Londa Alderink, Karen Campbell, Michael Ranville, Kristie Fry, Jay Howver, Roni Meek, and Carla Barnhill. From a don't-know-how-we-would-do-life-without-them standpoint, we are grateful for the long-suffering of our families and friends. And, of course, our dogs, Noel and Molasses.

Mirrors and Maps
An Introduction from Sissy

Last fall Melissa and I took a 400-mile road trip with our friend Mimi—on our bikes. No, we're not crazy and we're not super athletic. We're actually kind of normal and a lot like you, only older. And being older made it harder.

I cried a lot—pretty much every day—because I couldn't keep up with my friends. I had pictured the three of us riding alongside each other (which I later realized would have taken up a lot of space on the road and been illegal), singing songs, telling stories, and laughing together. But it wasn't quite like that.

Melissa flew several miles ahead of me at all times. Mimi stayed close to the middle, trying to decide if she should keep up with speeding Melissa in the front or check on weeping Sissy in the back. Humongous RVs with names like "The Crusher" blew past us every few miles. There were way more uphills than downhills, and for long stretches it felt as if we were riding our bikes over a metal cattle grate instead of a road. And did I mention it was 400 miles, which equaled 40 miles a day for 10 very long days? Okay, maybe we were a little crazy.

But some little pushes along the way made the ride easier. We had different friends follow along in cars and provide us with drinks and snacks. Most of our snacks were healthy and gave us much-needed energy. They were all helpful, but the caramel brownies helped the most. Reaching mile 40 each day helped, too. Music made a huge difference—especially songs like "I Will Survive" and "We're All in This Together." And friends definitely did their part. Three of our friends made goofy signs and taped them to trees and bridges along the way to encourage us and make us laugh. At one point they sat on top of hay bales in a field, holding their signs and cheering us on as we passed.

All of that stuff was important, but we couldn't have made it through the trip at all if it weren't for two travel essentials. Before we left, we had rearview mirrors attached to our bikes. These mirrors helped us see if we were about to be run over by The Crusher, and sometimes they helped Melissa and Mimi see that I was nowhere in sight. But they also inspired us by showing us what we'd accomplished so far. There's nothing like looking back at the hill you've just climbed to remind you of how strong you really are. Those mirrors quickly became indispensable.

We also came to rely on the mile markers. If you haven't been on a marathon bike trip like ours and don't know what mile markers look like, they are signposts along the side of the highway telling you how many miles you are from the beginning—or end—of the road. They were like a real-life map of the route we rode. Sometimes the mile markers were all we could think about: *Okay, we just passed mile marker 237. Only 26 miles to go. 25. 24*—you get the picture. The mile markers reminded us how far we had come and how far we had left to go to reach our destination.

This time in your life is a lot like our 400-mile bike ride. You'll have all kinds of fun and beautiful surprises along the way. Some moments will make you laugh, and some moments are so exciting you can hardly contain your joy. But other times life is just a hard ride. Some older girls will tell you the years between ages 11 and 14 were the hardest stage of growing up for them.

Of course you'll have great days during these years, lots of them. But then you'll have the other days, the days when you wake up feeling lousy about yourself for no apparent reason, the days you're mortally embarrassed by your parents, the days when all you want is to be part of the popular crowd. These are days when the questions bouncing around in your head have you so overwhelmed and confused you don't know how you're ever going to make it through the next hour.

Maybe you're wondering how we know what's going on in your head. Well, when we're not biking our legs off, we spend our days with girls a lot like you. We're counselors who talk to girls every day about the stuff they struggle with and worry about. We listen to them as they wrestle with issues like friendship, boys, peer pressure, their relationships with their parents, and their relationships with God. And we've found that nearly all of them ask four basic questions, questions you might be asking, too:

- Who am I?
- What do I want most in my life?
- What should I do?
- Who do I want to be?

This book is our way of helping you with these questions. We'll share our ideas about what you're going through and how you can manage all of it. And we'll introduce you to some of the girls we know who are on the same journey you're on. You'll also hear from girls who are a little farther up the road and find out what they've learned along the way. You'll find their words in little quotes throughout the book.

We also want to give you those two essential travel tools that made our bike trip so much better: First we'll give you a rearview mirror so you can see where you've been and take stock of all God has done in your life up to this point. Then we'll give you a map—a set of mile markers—to guide you as you find your way through this sometimes-bumpy part of life. This book is our way of riding alongside you, giving you caramel brownies, and holding up signs to make you laugh as you take the glorious journey of becoming the person God made you to be.

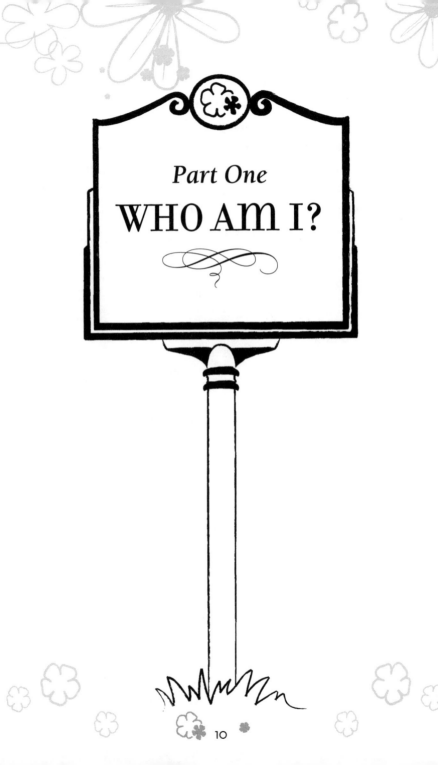

Part One

WHO AM I?

1

Mile Marker One:
we're not in kansas anymore

You've probably seen—or at least heard of—*The Wizard of Oz*. So you know the deal: Dorothy, a girl about your age, is trying to escape a tornado and a crazy, witchy woman who wants to take her cute little dog, Toto. She runs into her room to hide and gets hit on the head and knocked out. When she wakes up, she opens the door to walk outside and finds the world has changed. Everything on her aunt and uncle's farm had been dreary, gray, and dusty—viewers see that part of Dorothy's life in black and white. But the world she enters is sunny and bright—almost too bright. Munchkins are coming out of enormous flowers, and a beautiful witch is floating down from the sky in a pink bubble.

As you can imagine, Dorothy is a little thrown. She turns to her dog and says, "Toto, I have a feeling we're not in Kansas anymore." And she's right.

These years of your life are a lot like Dorothy's waking up in Munchkinland. You're going along, minding your own business, playing with your dog, trying to stay out of trouble—when all of a sudden, you wake up and everything is different.

You used to like to go to movies with your parents; now it's embarrassing. You used to want to hang out in the family room; now you'd rather be in your own room with the door shut. The computer is more fun than your bike or Barbies, and friends are more important than just about anything else. The world has gone from black and white to color—and it's very confusing.

I (Sissy) was talking to a friend of mine who just started the fifth grade. I asked her how fifth grade was different from fourth. She said, "It's totally different. I don't know why, but all of a sudden, your friends are *really* important. Everyone hugs each other when they see each other at school like we haven't seen each other in years. You used to like your friends and want to play with them, but not like this. What they think really matters—especially what they think about you. And you want to talk to each other and be together all the time. It's really weird."

It is really weird, or at least really different from how you felt and acted just a few years—or even a few months—ago. But those of us who've gone through this stage already would say it's really normal. And it all has to do with your development.

Development: The Door to Oz

Up until now your development has been something that just kind of happened. But now you're probably starting to notice the ways you're changing. And you're noticing the ways people around you are changing, too. So while you haven't given much thought to your development, you've likely thought about how some girls are getting meaner and some boys are getting cuter. You've thought about how different you feel on the inside—and look on the outside. And like our friend said, you've thought a *lot* about what other people think about you. All of this is part of living in the land of development.

The years between ages 11 and 14 bring on all kinds of

changes. Some changes are physical—you'll look pretty different at 14 than you did at 11. Other changes happen inside, in your emotions and your spiritual life. All this change can sometimes be hard to understand. And that's where we think we can help.

Change is a natural part of growing up—believe it or not, most of what you're experiencing is part of God's design for you. That means none of these changes are random. There are physical reasons you wake up feeling bad about yourself sometimes. There are emotional reasons friends are so important. And there are spiritual reasons your thoughts about God and about life don't make sense quite the way they used to.

So we're going to talk a little bit about all of this development business. And we're going to talk specifically about what happens for a lot of girls between the ages of 11 and 14.

Your experiences might be a bit different from the experiences we'll talk about in this book. Some of the things that happen to 11-year-olds might've happened to you when you were nine or may not happen until you're 16. That's normal. God designed every girl to be different. So there's nothing wrong with you if you start your period when you're 10 or you don't really care much about boys until you're 16. It just means all of these changes are happening at the speed God wired into you.

But I Kind of Like Kansas

You might read all of this and think you want God's timing for you to grow up to be—never. Maybe you have a teenage sister who fights with your parents all the time, and you don't want to be like that. Maybe you really like playing with your dolls and stuffed animals and are afraid you'll have to give that up. Or maybe you're anxious about starting your period or wearing a bra or all of the other body changes you know are coming.

Well, we have good news. No, you can't put off becoming a teenager or skip over the hard parts. But a lot about being a teenager is great, too. This is the time in your life when you're becoming more of who God made you to be. You're discovering you have thoughts and feelings of your own, not just echoes of your friends' or parents' ideas. You're finding out what you're good at and what gets you excited. You're getting more independent, more responsible, and more grown-up. And while it can be a little scary to think about shifting from being a little girl to being a teenager and, eventually, an adult, the really great news is—you don't have to let go of all the fun parts of being young. After all, Sissy gets excited about her Nintendo Wii, and Melissa loves to ride her bike. Growing up doesn't mean turning into someone else. It means figuring out how the girl you've been will become the grown-up God created you to be.

So even though leaving Kansas may sound a little scary— and will be at times—you have so much to look forward to as you step into Oz. Dorothy's journey took her past trees that grabbed her and monkeys that attacked her. But she also found friends who loved her and courage she didn't know she had.

Your developmental journey will look a lot like Dorothy's. You may be battling mean girls instead of monkeys (although they can seem pretty similar) and your own insecurities instead of trees, but you'll make it through. With good friends, courage, and a little help from us, we think you'll finish the ride with more confidence and a better sense of yourself than when you started.

2

Mile Marker Two:
REMEMBER WHEN... (BIRTH TO 10)

Melissa was a really cute little girl, the kind of cute that made her seem sort of defenseless. She had red hair, an adorable smile, glasses, and big blue eyes—one of which crossed from time to time. If you had seen her sitting at her desk in class, you would've wanted to protect her from any kid who tried to tease or bully her.

Well, maybe not. Billy, a boy in her fourth-grade class, would tell you Melissa didn't need any protection. In fact, Billy learned the hard way that nobody messed with Melissa.

Billy must've thought Melissa was cute, too, because he decided to chase her around the playground (that's the fourth-grade-boy way of saying, "I kind of like you"). Well, Melissa did what most fourth-grade girls would do—she ran. Day after day, recess after recess, Melissa ran, trying to stay away from Billy.

But one day something dawned on Melissa. She didn't have to run. That day Billy came around the corner—running full blast—only to find Melissa standing there in her pink dress, hands on her hips, staring straight at him. And do you know what brave Billy did? He turned around and ran in the other direction.

Armed with her newfound confidence, Melissa started doing the chasing. She chased Billy all over the playground until she finally caught him. And Melissa not only caught Billy, but she also caught him so forcefully she landed on top of him and broke his arm.

Even if you weren't chasing boys and breaking their arms on the playground, you were a lot like Melissa when you were younger. From the time you were a baby until now, you've had the strength to run—not actual running, but running with your ideas, your dreams, and your imagination. You've had the confidence to believe you could conquer the world.

But you're also aware you've had some weaknesses over the years—difficult times and situations that might still affect you today. Maybe you've got a short temper or you're impatient or you've struggled to make friends. All of this—the strengths and the weaknesses—is part of being a human.

Remember that bike trip we took? The times when we were working every muscle in our bodies to get our bikes up steep hills seemed as if they'd never end. We'd complain and grunt and even cry (okay, only Sissy cried) about the miserable uphill parts of the ride. But we also had times when we'd find ourselves at the top of a hill, knowing we were about to take a free-flying downhill run. We'd lean back, let the wind cool us off, and use gravity to rest our legs and enjoy the ride.

Growing up is filled with uphills (the hard times) and downhills (those times when life feels easy). If you think about it, you can probably look at your life so far and see a few uphills and a few downhills. The truth is, every stage of life has a mix of the two. And just like our little rearview mirrors helped us look back at the hills we climbed on that bike trip, this chapter will help you look back at the uphills and downhills of the first 10 years of your life.

Maybe you're wondering why we're talking about the uphills and downhills already behind you. Maybe you'd rather just forget about all of that "little girl" stuff and move on. But looking back isn't about reliving the past. It's about learning more about yourself and remembering who you are and where you've been. Because when you look back, you can have a better understanding of where you are now and where you might be going next.

The Uphills

We're going to talk about the uphills first, mostly because we're both "eat-your-vegetables-before-your-ice-cream" kind of people. That means we'd rather get the hard things over with so we can enjoy the easy stuff. The uphills in your first 10 years can be pretty tough—tough to go through at the time and tough to get over later. But we believe most girls have struggled with similar issues in their first 10 years. We know you might have had other tough uphills, like your parents' divorce or kids making fun of you at school, and we'll talk about those kinds of uphills in a few chapters. But for now we want to talk about two major uphills we know lots of girls struggle with and exactly what you can do about them.

Watch me!

Have you been around any little girls lately? Maybe you've seen them at the pool or the park. Maybe you have a younger sister. Maybe a neighbor girl likes to hang around with you once in a while. If you know any younger girls, then you've probably noticed they're often looking for attention. They stand at the top of the diving board or the slide or the steps and shout, "Mommy [or Daddy or whoever they're trying to impress], watch me!" Well, believe it or not, you did the same thing. "Watch me!" is a favorite saying for kids in their single-digit years, and we bet it was one of yours. You may not remember saying the words, but you can probably remember how badly you wanted your mom to see your drawings, your dad to watch you swing, or your teacher to watch you do a cartwheel.

Whether you were drawing, swinging, or tumbling, your mom or dad or grandparents or whoever would witness your newest feat of excellence would say something like, "Way to go, honey. That was fantastic!"

Even though you're older now, the shouts of "way to go" are just as important. You might act like it doesn't matter whether people are proud of you, but most girls we know still long for the people they love to notice their accomplishments. You probably don't shout, "Hey, Mom, watch me get great grades!" whenever you come home with a new report card. And you probably don't turn to your dad when you score a goal in a soccer game and yell, "Watch me be the star soccer player!" That might be a little bit of overkill. But you still want to be noticed.

And that's okay. We all want attention. We want admiration and respect and love. We all want the adults in our lives to delight in us. But as you get older, those dramatic acts meant to get attention can actually turn people away from you rather than toward you.

Maybe you know someone who brags a lot. It might be about her grades, her dad's job, or how many friends she has. Basically, she's saying, "Watch me!" to anyone and everyone who will listen. If you know someone like this, you also know how it feels to have to listen to her attempts to get attention.

So now you've got two competing needs. You don't want to be the girl other people are tired of, but you still want and need to be noticed—to have people pay attention to you. So how do you do that without being annoying?

Easy. The best way to get the delight and attention you want is to be you. Just being who you are—with no bragging to get attention, no acting up or acting out, no practical jokes, no drama—is enough for you to be adored. How do we know? Because God already adores you. Here's what the Bible says about God's feelings for you: "The LORD your God is with you, the Mighty Warrior who saves. He will take great delight in you; in his love he will no longer rebuke you, but will rejoice over you with singing" (Zephaniah 3:17).

Even though you know God adores you, it can sometimes feel as if no one else does. And that can make life hard. But remember, everyone else feels that way sometimes—we'll tell you why in the next chapter. So if your friends aren't paying attention to you, it's not because they don't like you; it's because they're worried no one likes them. It's easy for us to get so focused on what other people think about us or how they treat us we forget to think about how we're treating others.

You are loved and delighted in by God. And we would guess a few others would line up to tell you how great they think you are, too. That's a wonderful feeling. But it also means you have a responsibility to care for other people that way—by telling your friends how great they are. Show some love and kindness to your family. One of the best ways to stop worrying about the amount of attention you're getting is to give your attention and love to someone else who needs it.

Fears

Were you afraid of the dark when you were younger? Were you afraid there were monsters under your bed? In your closet? We have a friend named Molly. When she was in elementary school, she would jump onto her bed from several feet away so the monsters couldn't grab her ankles.

We also have a friend named Aubrey who got sick every time her mom went to work. The fear of something happening to her mom physically affected Aubrey's body. When you were younger, you may have had imaginary fears like Molly or more realistic fears like Aubrey (and maybe you still have some of those fears). It doesn't really matter what you were afraid of. The fear was real to you and it was pretty awful.

If you've ever seen a VeggieTales movie, you might remember a song about fear called "God Is Bigger Than the Boogeyman." The boogeyman can be the monster you think is under your bed or the witch you think is in your closet. It may be your parents getting in a car accident or something happening to you while you're at school. God is bigger than all of those boogeymen who scared you when you were younger.

Today you might have a new set of fears—other girls gossiping about you, being left out, or your parents getting divorced. Whatever scares you, remember God is bigger than your worst fear.

The book of Psalms in the Bible is made of prayers and poems and songs, most of them written by a man named David. David faced all kinds of scary things in his life—battling a giant, being the king during a war, having his son die. So he knew how it felt to be really, truly afraid. He wrote, "When I get really afraid I come to you in trust. I'm proud to praise God; fearless now, I trust in God. What can mere mortals do?" (Psalm 56:3-4, MSG) And, "Say this: 'God, you're my refuge. I trust in you and I'm safe!' That's right—he rescues you from hidden traps, shields you from deadly hazards. His huge outstretched arms protect you—under them you're perfectly safe; his arms fend off all harm" (Psalm 91:2-4, MSG). And in the book of 1 John, John writes, "There is no fear in love. But perfect love drives out fear" (4:18).

With God in your life, you can leave those fears—both real and imagined—behind. God is bigger than they are.

That doesn't mean you'll never face another uphill. It means God will be beside you on those tough climbs, giving you love, comfort, confidence, peace, and the strength to make it through to the next downhill ride.

The Downhills

Now for the good parts. Even during those hard times, God was doing some really cool things inside of you—physically, emotionally, and spiritually—in those first 10 years. God was placing gifts and strengths inside of you to help make up who you are today.

Wired for friendship

An old song called "Anything You Can Do I Can Do Better" from the musical *Annie Get Your Gun* is sung by the two main characters, Annie Oakley and Frank Butler. In the song Annie and Frank are competing with each other to see who's better at all kinds of things—from singing to shooting to shopping.

During the first 10 years of her life, Annie would've been right about being better than Frank. Young girls can do a lot that boys the same age can't. Each of these things has to do with one of the parts of the female brain growing faster than the same part in the male brain. These differences still affect you today. Here's what we mean:

What You Could Do	Inside Your Brain	What It Meant Then	What That Means Now
• Talk earlier	• The left hemisphere of the brain controls speech—a girl's left hemisphere grows more quickly.	• This one is kind of easy: You could talk earlier than boys your age.	• In an average day you probably spend more time on the phone or talking to people than your guy friends.
• Control your emotions and responses	• Girls' brains create more serotonin, which has to do with impulse control. The limbic system—the part that manages emotions—also develops faster in girls than in boys.	• Your guy friends probably got into trouble more than you did in elementary school. They would have trouble stopping themselves from yelling or poking other boys—or you.	• Boys have a harder time controlling their feelings and impulses, while you have a little more control over how you express your emotions.
• Recognize different sights, smells, sounds, and feelings	• The occipital lobe—the part of the brain that takes in information—develops earlier in girls.	• Girls can be aware of lots of different things—and feelings—going on around them all at the same time.	• You can watch television, text message one friend, and be on the phone with another—all at the same time. Boys typically have to focus on one thing at a time.
• Remember more and in greater detail	• The hippocampus, which controls memory, develops more quickly in a girl's brain.	• You couldn't wait to get home from school and tell your mom every detail you remembered from your day—who played with you at recess, what grade you got on your spelling test, and on and on and on.	• Guys remember the big picture while you remember every detail of a story—who was wearing what, who was standing where, who said what, and even who looked at who a certain way.

This list doesn't exactly describe everyone. It just shows what generally happens for girls and boys. Some boys' brains grew faster than a lot of girls'. But for the most part, you and Annie Oakley could shoot and shop and sing better than the guys—and you could do it all at the same time.

One more important activity was going on in your young brain. It has to do with something called oxytocin. Oxytocin is a chemical swimming around in your brain. This chemical is what makes you want to take care of things like stuffed animals and baby dolls. If you have a baby one day, it will help you give birth and create milk for your child. Boys produce oxytocin, too, but not nearly as much as girls (obviously, they don't need it quite as much).

Here's what oxytocin does. Melissa's nieces Mady and Libby and their brothers Sam and John all got dolls for Christmas when they were little. Their mom wanted all of her kids—the girls and the boys—to be able to play with dolls if they wanted. You can probably guess what happened. Mady and Libby cuddled with their dolls, brushed their hair, and dressed them—probably the same things you did with your dolls. Sam and John played with their dolls, too. They put them in toy cars and drove them off cliffs. They blew them up. This is oxytocin (and the lack of it) at work.

God specifically made girls to care for and about others. He designed you to care about friends and your parents. He created you to love other people and to want to be loved back. From the time you were a brand-new baby, you were made to be in relationships with other people. And relationships, as hard as they can be sometimes, are some of the great downhills of life.

Confidence

You might not be feeling very confident these days. Worrying might be much more natural for you. And how could you not worry when you've got one friend who's mad at you, a girl who is supposedly your friend talking behind your back, a cute boy who doesn't seem to notice you're alive, grades to worry about, and a million other pressures that bombard you as soon as you walk into school every day? How can you be confident in the face of all that?

But those things didn't used to matter so much. Do you remember when you first started playing basketball or soccer? You would run the wrong direction and just laugh. Or think about when you first learned to play the piano or the flute. If you messed up, you didn't worry that everyone was watching you. You just started again. Those moments of learning took confidence—and confidence was a natural part of your first 10 years.

That confidence went hand-in-hand with all the learning you did during those first 10 years. Maybe you don't think you learned much, but consider everything you accomplished even before you turned 10: You learned to crawl, walk, talk, read, and write. Many of you learned to ride a bicycle, play board games, and do handstands. You might have learned to hit a tennis ball or draw a horse. You could have learned to

> *I am a senior in high school and proud to say that I have—for the most part—conquered my fears. Exactly how I did it I couldn't really tell you. It took several long conversations with God before I was able to convince myself that my fears were not real— and several more before I was willing to turn out my closet light without checking to make sure the closet was empty first. Slowly but surely, I handed my fears over to the Lord and trusted that he would take care of both them and me. Fear was just a tool Satan used slowly to build a brick wall between myself and God, and with God's promise never to leave me or forsake me, I slowly began tearing down that brick wall.*
> —Elizabeth

swing a bat or sing in a children's choir. You might have even learned to speak a different language.

That's a whole lot to learn at any age, let alone when you're a young girl. Read back over the list up there. That's enough to make you feel pretty confident in yourself. And as if that weren't enough, you were also learning how to find friends and how to keep friends. You were learning how to make other kids laugh, how to talk to adults, and how to make your teacher smile.

All that learning developed your personality—with all the strengths and abilities, characteristics and gifts that are important parts of who you are today. That's why you spent countless hours practicing piano. It's why your mom made you invite the people who weren't your best friends to your birthday parties. It's why you had to write endless thank-you notes and talk to adults even when you didn't remember who they were. The more you did all of this, the more you developed those strengths and abilities, characteristics and gifts.

But it's harder to feel confident now. You resist trying activities you've never tried because you're worried you'll look silly. You hesitate to make new friends because you worry they won't like you. You avoid talking to adults because you feel like a goofy kid. But that's what's so great about those strengths and gifts—they don't leave you. You're still the same girl who mastered the violin or learned to write in Spanish or figured out how to do multiplication. Your confidence might feel as if it's faded away, but we promise, it's still there. And no amount of gossiping girls or mean boys or struggles in school or sports can take it away from you.

Awareness

"He called a little child, whom he placed among them. And

he said: 'Truly I tell you, unless you change and become like little children, you will never enter the kingdom of heaven. Therefore, whoever takes a humble place—becoming like this child—is the greatest in the kingdom of heaven.'" (Matthew 18:2-4)

We have a little friend named Mary Holland. Actually, she's very little—she's two. She's the only girl in a family of five children. And she hates it when her brothers get in trouble. Much to her mom's dismay, every time one of the boys is in time-out, Mary Holland brings him her favorite stuffed lamb to hold. Sometimes she even tries to give him a snack. She's only two, but Mary Holland knows when her brothers are sad and wants to help them feel better.

We've heard story after story about little girls like this. One girl met a boy who was in a wheelchair, invited him to her house, and fed him popsicles. Another girl wrote a letter, with no prodding from her mom, to a woman whose husband had just died. Another girl tried to comfort her soccer teammates when they weren't playing well. These girls were aware of the needs of those around them. And we think that's one of the reasons Jesus told people to be like children.

As you've gotten older, it's become a little harder to have this kind of awareness of others. You're much more aware of what people are saying about you or might be thinking about you. You're very aware of your feelings, but it's like your brain is way too busy to be aware of the feelings of others. Still we believe being aware of others is part of the humility Jesus is talking about in Matthew 18. This awareness is an essential part of love and compassion—the ability to feel concern for other people.

It's pretty easy to be aware of and compassionate toward your closest friends. But it's also easy to get so focused on yourself that you don't really notice the feelings of other people. Maybe your parents or siblings have started to accuse you of being selfish. Well, one of the reasons teenagers are often called selfish is because they temporarily lose their sense of awareness.

Becoming aware means allowing yourself to see the needs of people—all people, not just your very best friends. Your mom might need you to wash the dishes. A girl at school might be sitting

I wish I had known that other people's lives don't revolve around mine.
—Monique, 17

by herself in the lunchroom. All kinds of people in your life need compassion and love.

During the first 10 years of their lives, most girls are described as "sweet" by their parents. Most teenage girls aren't. You can change this. You can love others the way God wants us to by being aware of the needs of others and reaching out to them with compassion.

All of these wonderful parts of you—your perfectly wired brain, your basic confidence, your ability to notice the needs of other people—have been working together since you were a baby. They've created those fantastic downhill times in your life. They're what made being a little kid so much fun. You were fearless. You were kind. You were able to learn and grow and change because that's how God made you.

When you use the rearview mirror to look back at your life so far, you can see all the uphills and downhills you've survived already. If it's hard to remember what you were like during those first 10 years, ask your parents. Have them tell you stories about your early years. Watch home movies. Visit your grandparents and ask them to tell you about the things you used to love to do or things you were afraid of. As you listen and watch, you'll see glimpses of who you are and who

God is growing you to become.

Think About It
What helped you feel confident when you were younger?

What things chipped away at your confidence?

How do those experiences continue to affect who you are today?

Describe some parts of you God was developing in those first 10 years.

Write down three of your favorite childhood memories.

What do these memories tell you about yourself or other people in your life?

3

Mile Marker Three:
THE CALM BEFORE THE STORM... (11 AND 12)

Do you like to be out in a thunderstorm? Not really outside (that would be a little silly), but maybe on your screened-in porch or peering out the window? I (Sissy) used to love sitting on the porch with my dad, watching rainstorms roll in. The clouds would slowly build. The wind would blow a little stronger. The air would start to smell different. And then would come this window of time when everything would get really dark, really still, and really quiet. The storm was coming, but it wasn't quite there. It was almost as if God was giving us a few minutes of warning before the real storm came so we could get ready.

Remember—a lot of older girls will tell you seventh and eighth grades were the hardest grades they ever went through. That's the storm, and although God does some great things in the midst of the storm, it can still feel like you're living in the middle of an emotional, physical, and spiritual hurricane. But the ages of 11 and 12 are the calm before that storm. The clouds have gathered. Your perspective is different. You're deeper, more thoughtful, more sensitive, but you still feel a freedom that won't come so easily in a few years. This is your time to get ready for the storm.

We recently asked a group of fifth and sixth graders what they were most worried about. Here's what they said:

• Crying in front of people

- Going through more physical changes than boys
- Shaving, starting my period, doing my hair
- Being bullied and yelled at in school
- Trying not to talk behind people's backs
- Trying to figure out boys
- Homework
- Relationships
- Grades
- Getting in trouble

These aren't the answers a second grader—or even most fourth graders—would give. These answers show something is different. These girls have a new kind of awareness. They're noticing things around and inside themselves they never noticed before. They're thinking about friends, bodies, and boys in a totally different way.

While these years are a time of getting ready for what's coming, they're also filled with plenty of uphills and downhills of their own. So not only are you preparing for the next stage of your life, but you're also trying to make it through this one. It's a lot to handle, but remember: You can do this. Look in your rearview mirror and remember all you learned in your first 10 years. See? You have what it takes to make it and even discover some new things about yourself.

The Uphills

The uphills during these years are more challenging than ever, but you can learn a lot along the way to carry you through the storm to come.

Puberty

We know. You would probably rather not read this section. It's a little bit like your mom sitting down and reading you a book about your changing body. In other words, it's embarrassing. But we're talking about it for the same reasons your mom wants to talk about it—because this can be a really stormy time in your life, and we want you to be ready for it.

Puberty is actually an uphill and a downhill—and then another uphill and another downhill, over and over again. So we're going to talk about both parts of the journey. Puberty means your body is going through a lot of changes. You're growing in places you never grew before (we'll come back to this later). You're feeling emotions you've never felt before. You're asking questions you've never asked before. As dorky as it sounds, all of the changes in your body mean you're becoming a woman.

The changes in your body are easy to see. But all kinds of change is going on in your brain, too. Your normal, growing brain has been kidnapped by something called hormones. Now hormones are great things. They make you feel good about yourself, help you enjoy your relationships, and make you want to take care of others—at least they will after puberty (and sometimes, every once in a while, you'll feel some of that during puberty). For now the hormones are trying to get themselves situated. They know they have important jobs to do, but the process of working out how and when to do it can be a little crazy. It's almost like having lots of little Tasmanian devils whirling around inside your brain.

Michael Gurian, a psychologist who has studied this kind of thing, wrote a book called *The Wonder of Girls*. He made a list of all the aspects hormones affect in girls going through puberty:
- Your moods
- The words you use, the speed of your conversation,

your need for conversation

- How you do on tests when you're having or about to have your period
- How much you eat
- How you relate to people nonverbally (without saying a word)
- How you feel about the people you love
- How you see yourself fitting in
- Your self-esteem
- Your desire to make friends
- Emotions like anger, joy, and sadness (Gurian, 38, 78-79)

Kind of overwhelming, huh? Hormones affect just about everything but the color of your eyes. Now this list isn't meant to get you off the hook when you've messed up on a test or yelled at your little brother. But it can help you have a better sense of why puberty can make you feel as if you're not yourself.

When you start having your period, you'll discover your hormones are particularly busy. That means a lot of your feelings about things on the list get even stronger during your period. You'll have days when you feel as if no one likes you. When these days come, look at the calendar; the chances are good you're about to start your period. The Tasmanian devils are causing you to feel and think about things in an exaggerated way—those feelings and thoughts don't reflect the reality of how your friends feel about you. If you don't do so well on a test or can't quit crying or seem to want to argue with your mom for no reason, your period may be the cause. We want you to remember this because it's so easy to start feeling bad about yourself when these things happen. It's easy to think you're a failure in school or you'll never have any friends or your mom hates you. But it's most likely your hormones talking.

Puberty is a tough stage to go through. And while all the hormonal craziness is no excuse for being unkind or disrespectful, it helps to remember hormones can make you feel and do things that are out of character for you. So try not to get too stressed out about the chaos you sometimes feel inside. Pretty soon those little devils will settle down, and you'll start feeling a lot more like yourself again.

Sensitivity

One of the big changes girls notice during puberty is that they become supersensitive. Have you noticed you cry more than you used to? When you were younger, you would fall down and get a little scrape or someone would say something mean to you and you'd be upset. You would probably run to your mom or dad, cry for less than a minute, then go right back to what you'd been doing.

Now if someone hurts your feelings, you can't stop thinking about it. Sometimes you want to talk to someone about it. Other times you want to go in your room, be by yourself, and think. Either way, the hurt doesn't go away as quickly or as easily as it used to. You feel it more deeply and for a lot longer.

You've become more sensitive for a couple reasons. The big one is hormones. They have just as much to do with your emotions as they do with the physical changes you see. Hormones act like magnifying glasses, making every feeling bigger and stronger than it used to be.

The other reason has to do with the whole Munchkinland thing we talked about in Mile Marker One. You see everything differently now. When you were seven, a friend could hurt your feelings by saying something mean. But if she wanted to play with someone else, you didn't think much of it. If she sat next to another kid during lunch, it was no big deal. These days those hurtful words and actions from others feel more personal—someone doesn't want to be your friend anymore, likes another girl better, or thinks you dress weird. Instead of just moving on to the next thing, you just want to go to your room, close the door, and worry.

In our counseling offices we talk about feelings on a scale from one to 10. One would be something that hurts your feelings a little, like your best friend can't hang out with you because she's already got plans with someone else. Five would be a little stronger, like she tells you she wants to hang out with someone else because she needs a little time away from you. Ten would be your best friend telling you she never wants to see or speak to you again. Get the picture?

We all get our feelings hurt. Some days are level-two days. Some days are level four. Every once in a while we hit an eight or a nine—hopefully not too often. But in the stormy years, everything feels like a 10—girls at this age just go there automatically. In part, that's because your hormones don't leave you much choice. But you also feel hurt so often because of this increased sensitivity.

It's the same idea of moving from black and white to color. Everything looks so different. You notice more. You're more aware of how people treat you—or don't treat you. You see how your friends treat each other. You even start to pay more attention to how your parents treat each other, which can be hard. You might even start to worry about your parents or your friends.

Even though your increased sensitivity means you'll get your feelings hurt more often, or the level-two hurts will feel more like 10s, this isn't only an uphill. It's actually a really great downhill, too. You can start to experience that compassion we talked about before because your strong feelings will help you understand the feelings of other people. You'll be able to care about others in ways that make you an even better friend.

And here's something else to keep in mind. When you feel so hurt you don't know what else to do but cry, you need to know God is there with you and can give you the comfort you need to start feeling better. The Bible tells us God knows when we're sad; God notices every tear and heartache. Psalm 56:8 says it's as though God collects our tears in a bottle and records each one in a book—just like you would do with your most important possessions and private thoughts. He cares about you that much.

> *Most girls have anxiety and get stressed. All girls have a tough life in some way. It hurts equally but about different things. No girl's life is perfect. There is always someone there who cares about you. Through God you are happier with your life than ever—happier than with the popular crowd, money, etc. Find friends who care about you, not your social status or how much attention you get.—Catherine, 14*

The extra sensitivity that comes with puberty can make for some tough days. But we promise you won't feel like this forever. In fact, you probably won't feel like this for long. So try your best to work through your hurt feelings by talking about them with a good friend or your mom or dad. Try not to hurt others when they've hurt you. And take advantage of your ability to notice the feelings of others by being a little kinder, a little more patient, and a little more compassionate.

Losing your voice

We love the show *American Idol*. In 2007 the winner was a 17-year-old named Jordin Sparks. We liked Jordin, but we really loved a girl with a huge smile named Melinda Doolittle.

We loved Melinda because she could sing her socks off. But we also liked her story. Melinda was actually tone-deaf until seventh grade—she couldn't sing on pitch at all. And then all of a sudden, she was able to sing. Her mom said it was a gift. Melinda made the most of that gift and became a background singer for some pretty famous folks—she went on national tours, recorded albums, met all kinds of big celebrities. But Melinda was never at the front of the stage. She was in the background, doing her thing out of the spotlight.

Then some friends persuaded her to try out for *American Idol*. She did, and week after week she made it to the next round. Every time she made it, she looked surprised and overwhelmed. Even Simon thought it was funny she was so surprised when it was obvious she had so much talent. But Melinda truly was surprised by the response to her voice. In one interview she talked about how the six steps from the background microphone to the front of the stage might not seem very far, but for her it was an awfully long walk.

What Melinda meant was: Stepping up to the front, being the person others were listening to and looking at, was scary. She was much more comfortable in the background. It was difficult for her to believe God really wanted to use her and her gifts.

So often in this calm before the storm, girls can fade into the background. You're feeling a lot of confusing emotions, and you're much more aware of the feelings of other people. All of this can make you lose some of the confidence you had in your first 10 years. And when that happens, you start letting other people—mostly your friends—think for you. You stop saying what you believe. You stop trying out for the main parts in the plays or raising your hand in class because you don't want to stand out. It's like losing your own voice—Melinda in reverse.

Okay, we know we've scared you half to death with all of this—don't worry; the good part is coming! As hard as the uphills can be, these years really are a time to enjoy your new awareness, look forward to becoming a young woman, and step up to that microphone. Have a voice. Stand up for what you believe. Say what you think—with the kindness that only comes from someone who's aware of others. Your voice can and does make a gigantic difference in this world. All you have to do is use it.

The Downhills

Now that we've terrified you about puberty, we want you to know really positive, long downhills are coming—a lot of them. The apostle Paul wrote about his own maturing process in a letter he wrote to some of his friends. He wrote, "When I was a child, I talked like a child, I thought like a child, I reasoned like a child. When I became a man, I put the ways of childhood behind me" (1 Corinthians 13:11).

All of the changes—even the ones involving the Tasmanian devils—mean you are leaving childhood behind. You're becoming a teenager, a young woman. This is an exciting, mysterious, wonderful time in your life.

Rather than our telling you all the terrific times you have to look forward to in the next few years, why don't we let the girls who are right in the middle of those years tell you?

"You get more freedom, and you learn more responsibility because of it."—Caitlin, age 19

"I am discovering who I truly am and what I want to stand for."—Chelsea, age 15

"People take me more seriously."—Erin, age 17

"People become less cliquey, and it's easier to find your really good friends."—Jessica, age 17

"My parents trust me more, and I'm more independent."—Sara, age 16

"I like the responsibilities that come because they help us grow closer together as friends...plus the girls get nicer!"—Hollis, age 15

"I have become closer to my mom in more of a friendship way instead of only a parent-child way."—Kathleen, age 19

"I know more who I am now—and don't care so much about trying to be the most popular or most whatever. I've figured out more of what I'm truly interested in and have friends to hold me accountable."
—Sandy, age 17

In these years of periods and puberty and everything else, you're becoming you. You're learning who you want to be, how you want to love other people, what you believe in and are passionate about, and what you believe God has created you to do.

Plus you get to do all kinds of exciting things like wear a bra, shave your legs, and wear deodorant. (Okay, maybe they don't sound so exciting now, but they are some of the fun perks of being a girl.) Even though the uphills will be pretty tough in the next few years, we believe they're well worth it as you discover the amazing person God has created you to be.

Puberty: The sequel
Believe it or not, there really are wonderful downhills to puberty.

From a science-book perspective, puberty is the transition from childhood to adulthood. That's going on inside you right now.

Physically, your body is growing up and out in new places. You're becoming curvy—which is a wonderful part of being a woman. You'll have days when you're not so sure you like these curves and think all they do is make your body look bigger. But curves are normal. They're part of being a woman. You might not think they look normal because so many of the models and celebrities in magazines look like they have no roundness to them. But that's because either their curves have been Photoshopped off, or the women you see are often unhealthy. Your curves mean you are healthy and beautiful—they're an important part of how God designed women.

Puberty also means you get hair in new places. And your body hair might not be like the body hair of your best friend. This is just one more way you're unique. There's nothing weird or wrong or abnormal about you if you need to shave your legs every day. There's nothing weird or wrong or abnormal about you if you only need to do it once a week—or don't want to do it at all.

You'll also notice as your menstrual cycle begins, you'll have days when you're really thoughtful and caring and other days when you're just the opposite. But even those shifting moods are powerful reminders that God made women to love and care and be in relationships.

Your period can still be confusing and kind of a hassle. You get cramps. Your back hurts. You might even get a little dizzy or nauseated around the time of your period. And you have to figure out how to use tampons and wear pads. (As embarrassing as it might be, you can ask your mom or your grandmother or your older sister to help you figure these out.) And it's really not nearly as bad as it seems. It only lasts a few days a month, and you'll have it figured out before you know it.

One day when you're much older and married, God might use all of these changes to help you conceive and create and care for a child. Your curves are more than lovely—they're the way your body protects a growing baby. And your menstrual cycle gets your body ready to nourish that baby until it's born. We know it's not always fun to deal with these changes, but when you think about how they all work together to prepare your body for the possibility of creating another life, it's pretty amazing.

A great movie called *Wide Awake* deals with this time in the life of a young teenager. The main character in the movie is a fifth-grade boy. At the end of the school year he gives a speech in front of his class. He looks back at the beginning of the year and talks about how he spent his time worrying about bullies, playing with friends, and wanting to be a superhero. He goes on to say that by the end of the year he was thinking about girls, how you sometimes lose the people you love, and how bullies were probably bullied themselves. He ends his speech with this great metaphor. He says it felt like he'd spent most of his life asleep, but now he was finally wide awake.

Puberty is the alarm clock that wakes you up—your feminine body, your hormones, your awareness, your emotions, and your concern for other people. Not only are you awake as puberty comes to a close, but you also have a more mature outlook on your life and the people in it. And all of that makes puberty a pretty cool downhill.

Thirst

We both get to spend our summers on the lake. From June to August we run a camp for kids called Camp Hopetown. Every morning and evening at camp, I (Melissa) talk about some theme from the Bible. Last summer we talked about thirst.

The Bible talks a lot about our being a thirsty people. What does that mean? Well, have you ever worried about being liked? Left out? Not being funny enough? Not being chosen for a team? Are you afraid you might not fit in or you're not good enough to please someone important to you? Do you know why you worry about those things? You guessed it—it's because you're thirsty.

God made you with a thirst to be loved and liked, to love others, and to know you make a difference to someone else. But you have an even deeper thirst than those. That's a thirst for God.

Our fifth-and-sixth-grade camp was a particularly powerful one last summer. Our worship was loud and rich, and it was obvious God was moving in the lives of the kids. Do you know why? Because they were thirsty.

The second-through-fourth-grade camp was fun. Those campers talked about God and understood God in simple, important ways. But fifth-and-sixth-grade camp was different. The storm clouds were gathering. These kids were starting to ask questions they'd never thought about before:

- "Why does God allow bad things to happen?"
- "Why do I want those girls to like me so much?"
- "How do you hear God talk to you?"

One night several of the counselors were meeting in my (Melissa's) room after the girls had gone to bed. Someone quietly knocked at the door. When I opened it, four girls filed into my room. They asked me to come back to their room and talk more about Jesus. Now this isn't because I'm such a great teacher. What they really wanted to do was talk—about the things they think and worry about and about how Jesus can be with them in all of that. They wanted to talk about their thirst and how Jesus can quench it.

Think About It

It's normal to be thirsty for relationships. You're thirsty to be close to others and to God. You're thirsty to be included and important. What else? Take a minute to write down some of the things you might be thirsty for.

Saying you're thirsty and what you're thirsty for is really telling God you need him. So take a few minutes—or more if you want—to write about what you're thirsty for. If you need some inspiration, take a look at what David wrote in Psalm 42:2. He says, "My soul thirsts for God, for the living God. When can I go and meet with God?" You can write out a prayer or write about your hopes and dreams for what your life will be like. Write about the things that worry you and make you anxious.

Then look over what you've written. What does it tell you about what's really important to you?

The Downhills, Continued
Freedom

We're writing this section during a ski trip. To be honest we're not great skiers. We have a lot of fun, but our fun takes place on the easiest slopes—the green and blue kind (ski resorts use color-coded markers to tell skiers how hard a hill is: Green for easy, blue for intermediate, black markers for difficult). Every once in a while, however, we find ourselves on a supposedly easy slope, but it seems to change colors halfway down. This happened to us just yesterday.

We were making our way down this beautiful, easy hill overlooking a valley when we suddenly found ourselves on a very steep—too steep for us—kind of hill. So we stopped for a minute to figure out if we could get down any other way—besides skiing down. As we were standing there, a group of 11-and-12-year-olds whizzed past us with their ski instructor.

"Everybody come over here," he shouted. "Do you all want to race to the bottom? I'll draw a line in the snow and count to three." And that's what he did. All those skiers, girls and boys alike, lined up, crouched low over their skis, tucked their poles up under their arms, and flew down the mountain in a blur before the instructor's "three" was out of his mouth.

The girls in the group weren't a bit concerned about what anyone thought of them. They were ready for the adventure of the race, and they felt the freedom to fly down that hill. Now if those girls had been 13 or 14, they probably wouldn't have been so quick to join in the race. They wouldn't have stooped quite so low over their skis because they would've wanted to see what the others were doing. They would've hung back a little to find out if their friends were really going to race. And they sure wouldn't have dared to go at full speed because they would never want their friends or the boys to see them fall. They would've been so concerned about what they looked like and what others might have thought about them that they would've hesitated to race, even if they really wanted to.

Maybe you've started to worry about this a little bit, too. But you'll most likely worry about it a lot more in the next few years. But for now you're still one of those girls who would race down the hill. You're still a girl who feels the freedom to do what you want without worrying about what others think. This is the calm before the storm.

Girls change at different speeds. Some of you will feel like 13-year-olds when you're 11. Others will feel like 11-year-olds when you're 15. That's a natural part of growing up— God designed each of us to grow in our own way. So whether you're already in the midst of puberty or wondering if you'll ever get some curves in your figure, remember you are wonderfully made just the way you are.

So be yourself. Use your voice. Step up to the microphone and sing your heart out. Share your heart and those new, deeper feelings with the people you love. Talk to your parents and grandparents. Ask your friends how they feel, especially when you notice they're sad. Be aware of the tough changes puberty brings and look forward to the great ones. Pay attention to your thirst and talk to God about it. God has given you so many gifts in these years before the storm, and he will bring even more in the years to come.

4

Mile Marker Four:
TEMPEST IN A TEAPOT (13 AND 14)

tem·pest (t_m′p_st) n.

1) *A violent windstorm, frequently accompanied by rain, snow, or hail.*

2) *Furious agitation, commotion, or tumult; an uproar.*

The tempest in my mind/Doth from my senses take all feeling else/Save what beats there (Shakespeare, King Lear, Act III, Scene IV).

Kind of looks like school, doesn't it? We just thought we'd scare you a little. Actually, we've been trying to think of different storm names—you know, to stick with our "Dorothy in Oz" and "calm before the storm" chapters. There are tornadoes, hailstorms, thunderstorms, hurricanes, snowstorms, and lots of other kinds of storms we're not scientific enough to know the names of. But as we were thinking about what it's like to be 13 and 14, the word *tempest* jumped out at us.

We didn't really know what it meant when we thought of it—other than that it's a kind of storm and sounds cool. But reading the definition, it fits perfectly. These years can feel violent at times. Some days life feels like rain, and some days it feels even worse, like hail. Then all of a sudden you have a great day, one that feels like a wonderful, beautiful snowfall.

Of course, the adults in your life might say during these years you're more like the second part of the definition—agitated, causing commotion and uproar. They feel furious; you feel furious. It's like living through Hurricane Teenage Girl.

But our favorite part of the definition up there is the quote by Shakespeare. Since he says the tempest inside takes all feeling from a person's senses, he understood (probably without meaning to) what it felt like to be a 13 or 14-year-old girl. This tempest of change is consuming. It messes with what you think and feel and want. It makes you question what other people think about you, how you look, what you're doing, what they're saying, and on and on.

Just for a minute, let's go back to those fifth-and-sixth-grade girls we talked to. Remember their answers for what they worried about the most? They had real concerns about friends and puberty and dealing with the changes in their lives. Now look at what a group of seventh-and-eighth-grade girls are worrying about:

- Gossip
- Having to get the right kind of clothes
- Other girls being critical
- Having to be someone you're not to fit in
- Always having to think about what you're going to wear, what other people are thinking, what someone said about you at school
- Girls talking about me
- Guys
- Peer pressure
- Emotional stuff (especially at that time of the month)
- If my friends are really going to be my friends around other people

- Rumors
- If I get in a fight with my friends, are we going to hate each other and become rivals?
- Mean friends
- Succeeding in school and in general
- Trying to be good at everything
- Trying to make myself worth someone's time
- Fighting with siblings
- Loneliness
- Messing up my life and not realizing it
- Worrying that people will think I'm weird
- Not making the right choices
- Gaining weight
- People judging me from my appearance
- Not knowing how to get out of a bad situation

Sounds like quite a tempest, doesn't it? Even reading the list makes it hard to think about anything else, except these worries. The thing is, some of these concerns are similar to the concerns of 11 and 12-year-olds—friends, bodies, boys. But even those that are kind of the same seem more intense, more serious. Now it's not just worrying whether other girls won't like you; you're worried about them being mean or gossiping or judging you. And you're not just worried about school or grades, but about how what you do right now will affect your future. The things you worry about when you're 11 and 12 are a big deal to you, but as you get older, the stuff that stresses you out seems like it just gets bigger.

The Uphills

We're not trying to make you panic—a lot is wonderful about these years, and we'll get to that soon. But first let's get through those uphills girls face at 13 and 14.

Self-Consciousness

A while back, I (Melissa) had a counseling appointment with a 14-year-old girl named Mary. I was just starting out as a counselor, and I was ready to help her. I knew whatever she was dealing with was going to be a really tough, complicated issue, and I was convinced I was the one to make it better.

Mary walked into my office. She was a beautiful girl with a smile that lit up the room. She sat down and immediately started talking: "I need you to help me with two things. I need you to make me skinny and funny. Then I know everyone will like me. Then my life will be perfect."

Now let's fast-forward to a much younger girl named Kathleen, who happens to be my (Sissy's) little sister. Kathleen was born when I was 16 and my parents were already pretty old (sorry, Mom and Dad). She was the delight of all of my parents' friends (whose children were teenagers by then) and my friends (who were teenagers themselves). She was adored. And she knew it.

One afternoon my mom was out running errands with Kathleen, who was three at the time. They stopped by the jewelry store where my mom set Kathleen (who was pretty cute and had a lisp that made her even cuter) up on the counter so she could keep an eye on her while she did whatever it was she was there to do. The woman who worked in the jewelry store asked Kathleen her name. My little sister said, "Well, my name is Kathleen, but most people call me thweetheart."

Now no 12-year-old—or 20-year-old or 50-year-old—on the planet would refer to herself as sweetheart (or thweetheart, for that matter). If she did, we'd think something was really wrong with her. But at three Kathleen had a confidence

Mary didn't. That's because Mary was living in the middle of a huge part of the tempest, a part we call self-consciousness.

When you were 11 and 12, you were starting to become aware of other people in a way you weren't before. Well, now at 13 and 14 that awareness is turning into a concern about what other people will think about you. You're so aware of their feelings (and mostly their feelings about you), you can't think of anything else.

Once again stuff going on in your brain is responsible for this self-consciousness. You see, your brain was growing a lot when you were little—nerve endings and synapses and all that stuff you're maybe learning about in science. But then it got very quiet for several years. The growing slowed way down—kind of took a break. But when you hit these stormy years, it took off again at super-speed. Your brain is making new connections all over the place—how to get all those hormones to do their thing, how to make decisions, how to process information, how to think about abstract ideas. It's a lot for the brain to do, and sometimes it gets overwhelmed.

Maybe this will help you picture what's happening in your head. People who live in older houses sometimes experience something called a short circuit. Someone might be drying their hair upstairs when all of a sudden, the lights go off downstairs. There was so much electricity needed at the same time, the house's electrical system couldn't handle it—so it gave up. Your brain does the same thing sometimes. All that growing gets to be too much, and your brain gives up. We call this a hiccup in confidence.

So you walk into school one day with everything fine and then—wham! The short circuit hits, and you feel like everyone is talking about you. Or you wake up feeling like your parents are really disappointed in you even though your report card was actually good. That lousy feeling is self-consciousness. It's the idea that any look, whisper, or comment out of the ordinary is about you. How often do you feel that kind of self-consciousness? If you're anything like nearly every other girl your age, probably a lot.

Most girls and guys your age experience this weird feeling because of something psychologists call an imaginary audience. When you get out of your mom's car at school, trip in front of the movie theater, or have on the same dress as someone else, it feels as if everyone around you is looking right at you. But here's the truth: The reason this is called an *imaginary* audience is because no one is really watching you. It only feels like it. The audience is truly imaginary.

What's hard to keep in mind during these years is, your feelings are sometimes going to fool you. What you feel is real, but it doesn't always reflect reality. So when you feel self-conscious, pay attention to the feeling. But then remind yourself: Just because you feel like everyone is looking at you doesn't mean they are. Or when you feel like everyone is mad at you, they probably aren't. They're worried that everyone else is watching them or upset with them. Your feelings aren't really coming from something that's happening out there—they're coming from those short circuits in your brain.

You may not believe being funny and skinny will solve all

> *I wish I'd known that it's absolutely okay to make mistakes and to change your mind as you go. And if you feel like you're constantly beating your head against a wall or pushing against a lot of resistance in a certain area of your life, it's probably because you're so busy following your own plan that you're blind to what God wants for you. And if it's always an uphill battle that you never seem to win, it's likely because you're not using your God-given strengths in whatever you're doing and because your plan for yourself and God's plan for you are not the same.—Raegan, 19*

your problems the way Mary did. But we would guess you think you need to be something you're not. That is self-consciousness, and it will make you forget the truth about who you are. Remember, you are loved. You are beautiful and wonderful in different ways from anyone else. So even though you probably won't go around calling yourself "thweetheart," you have every reason to be just as confident as you were when you were a cute little three-year-old.

Ambivalence

I (Sissy) used to ask my mom to come to my room and help me pick out a shirt to wear for school. I would hold out two for her to choose from. She would pick one, and I would put on the other one. I (Melissa) used to get my feelings hurt by friends and talk to my parents about it. I would ask their advice and then do exactly what I wanted.

Ambivalence. It's what's happening when you're sending two different messages to the people around you—particularly your parents—during these years. Messages like—

- Come close—get away.
- I need you—now leave me alone.
- Would you help me? I can do it.

You could probably continue this list with all the ways you want your parents to be part of your life and then want them to back off. That's ambivalence. It means having mixed feelings about someone or something. And it's no wonder those feelings are so mixed up right now. Part of you feels like a little kid—and wants to, at times. It's nice to have your mom come in and rub your back when you're sick or to know your dad is at the mall with you just in case you need him. At the same time, you're growing up, and you don't want to be treated like a child. You want to be respected for your opinions and ideas. You want to make your own decisions—no matter what time your parents want you to go to bed, you think it should be later. You want to have more time on the computer. You absolutely believe you need to have your own cell phone, your own television, your own room. Come close—get away. Ambivalence.

A few years ago, I (Sissy) was meeting with a girl named Natalie. All Natalie could talk about was how angry she was at her mom. The way Natalie described her mom; you would have thought the woman had horns and fire coming out of her nostrils. But one day I was with Natalie when her mom called to let her know she was there to pick her up. Natalie, angry Natalie, picked up the phone and said, "Hi, Mommy" in the most pleasant voice I'd ever heard her use. "Okay, I'm downstairs. See you in a minute. I love you." Natalie closed her phone, smiled at me innocently, and walked away. It wasn't a trick. Natalie genuinely loved her mom—and was furious with her on a regular basis.

Of course you want to be independent. And of course you have times when you still feel like a little girl. All of that is okay—and it's actually good for you to want both. This is the time in your life when you're learning how to think for yourself, what you want your life to be like, who you want to be. But your growing brain isn't quite ready to do all of that without the help of older people who love you and who want to see you be the best you possible. The uphill part is being patient in the middle of this ambivalence, patient with yourself and the people you are ambivalent toward (hint, hint—that means your parents).

Still this is an uphill because it affects those around you (like your parents) even more than it affects you. You can imagine—or at least we want you to try to imagine—what it feels like to be on the receiving end of this ambivalence. "Okay, she asked me to come to her room to help her pick out clothes. Then she picked the opposite from what I said. Why did she want me up there at all?"

Or, "She just told me to leave her alone. She said she doesn't ever want to talk to me again. Now she wants to know if I'll fix her favorite meal for dinner?" You can see where this could be a little frustrating.

It's part of the tempest. Thankfully, most adults know this (remember, they went through this storm, too) and will do their best to understand. But maybe you can go a little easy on them, too. This transition can feel pretty stormy for everyone involved.

Relationships

A friend of mine (Melissa's) once said relationships are the best and the worst things that ever happen to us. This is never truer than in seventh and eighth grades. That's why we've included several chapters in this book about relationships—why we want them, why they have the power to hurt us, and why they're so important to us. But we want to say a little bit about them here, too.

You're living the uphills of relationships every day. You know better than we do how important friends are to you. You want to have a group of friends to hang out with and a best friend to talk to. But groups have a habit of changing the rules about who gets to be in them and who doesn't—usually without warning and with no real reason behind the shift. And best friends sometimes like to trade each other in for new best friends—also with no warning and no reason. Friends are fickle, and they're at the height of their fickleness in seventh and eighth grades. They turn on you. Leave you out.

Flirt with the guy you have a crush on. And so on. It's because relationships are important and fickle that they can be more of an uphill than a downhill during these years.

You're in the middle of a storm. That storm can make you feel bad about yourself and your relationships. It can make you push your parents away and believe no one cares. But remember, the truth is not always what it seems or feels like. You are loved—and delighted in—by God and by others around you—and the tempest is really only in a teapot (we'll explain later!).

The Downhills
Independence

Do you remember how much you looked forward to being a teenager when you were younger? Do you have any idea why you did? Part of it was probably how movies showed teenagers—they were usually with groups of friends driving around in cool cars, with no parents anywhere around. Being a teenager meant a glamorous, fun-filled life of independence.

Now that you're actually a teenager, you know what it's really like. You have rules: You can't ride in a car with a friend until you're a certain age. You can't date until you're way past that age. You can't have boys in your room or talk on the phone or stay out past 10 o'clock. You probably have a bunch of other rules to keep you from living like a movie-star teenager. Those rules can be frustrating. But they're there to protect you, mostly from the not-so-glamorous, not-so-cool teenagers out there who make bad decisions, which can lead to terrible consequences. We know, we know. You might not agree. But we think the adults are right on this one.

And to be honest, that isn't really what independence is all about. Independence is you becoming your own person.

 58

It's about finding out who you are, discovering your opinions and ideas, beliefs, and values. What's great is, you can do all that and still be respectful of the rules given by adults around you.

In fact, your independence is exactly what parents want. Now it may make them nervous sometimes. But it is what they want. They want you to feel loved, smart, beautiful, and confident and have a faith that's meaningful to you. And they know you have to discover all of this on your own. Still, it's hard for the people who love you to watch you take risks and grow and learn and fail sometimes. They want to rush in and rescue you. And that can feel as if they're taking away your independence. It's not. It's parents being parents—protecting you, loving you, teaching you. That's what they do.

> *I wish I had known that no one can change me and there's always more than one side to a story.*
> *—Rachel, 16*

Independence comes through discovery. That's one of the reasons we want you to journal and read and talk to interesting people who you respect. Ask questions. Find out how the people you admire got to be the way they are. Ask them what lessons they've learned so far—what they wish they'd known when they were your age. Ask your parents, too. They have so much great insight to share with you—if you're willing to hear it.

And get to know new people, try new experiences, and look for things you might be interested in. If you want to know more about God, get involved with a youth group or ministry where you can grow and learn and struggle with other girls your age who are making good decisions. And write as much as you can. Writing helps you discover what you believe and why because it makes you put your thoughts down on paper.

Think About It

Take a few minutes to write down some things you want to learn more about.

How can you find out more about them?

Who can you talk to?

What books could you read?

What places in your community could you visit to find out more about these interests?

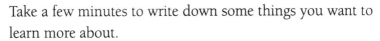

Start the discovery process—it helps you find out more about who you are and gain some independence all at the same time.

Independence, Continued

You have all kinds of ways to gain independence. Take a baby-sitting course and start baby-sitting for your neighbors. Try a new sport, a new kind of art project, or even a musical instrument. Learn to cook and surprise your family by making dinner. Two girls we know even started their own summer camp for three and four-year-olds in one girl's backyard. All of these experiences help build confidence and independence.

When we talk to girls your age, way too many of them say they let other people think for them. They lose their voices. Some of these girls are pushing hard against their parents' rules, saying they want independence. But they're just following someone else's idea of what it means to be independent. They're not becoming their own unique, amazing people. But you can. The best part of this exciting downhill ride is that you'll discover parts of yourself you never knew were there. You'll find the strength and wisdom and creativity to be the independent person you are, rather than someone other people think you should be.

Awareness

Allison is 14. Her parents have been married for a long time. She thought everything in her family was fine—until recently. She has started to notice her dad makes mean comments about her mom in front of other people. Her mom laughs and acts like it doesn't bother her, but Allison sees her mom spending more time by herself in her bedroom. She's worried that her mom is sad and her parents' marriage might not be as good as she thought.

This kind of noticing happens to a lot of girls your age. It might be happening to you. It could be your parents' marriage. It could be your mom seems to tell you what you're doing wrong a lot. Or your dad doesn't come home to have dinner with your family like other dads. It could even be something about your teacher or grandparents or aunts and uncles.

You're at an age where you're becoming much more aware of what's going on around you than ever before. Remember—your black-and-white world has just changed to color. You've been taught all your life that no one is perfect. Well, now you're seeing it. And you're even seeing it in people you've always looked up to, like your parents.

This is the hard part of awareness. You can start to notice other people's flaws and become disappointed in them, even critical. Or you can take this awareness and go a whole different direction. You can use it to increase the compassion we've been talking about. You can know being married is hard at times. When your parents are critical or do something wrong, you can talk to them about it (respectfully), and you can know we all mess up, you included. And you can start to learn that relationships take patience and kindness and understanding and forgiveness.

This might not seem like much of a downhill. In fact, it

sounds like kind of a lousy discovery. At times it is. It's hard to take off those kid goggles that make everything look easy and worry-free. But this awareness is definitely a downhill because it's a huge part of becoming an adult. Understanding other people, knowing relationships have good times and hard times, and learning how to forgive others are important parts of what it means to love. These are what you need to build friendships that last, to have a close connection to your family, even to develop good relationships with guys. It can be tough to start seeing people—your parents in particular—as real people with real struggles. But it's a major sign you're not in Kansas anymore.

Messiness

Several summers ago at the camp we run, I (Melissa) talked about pots. I don't mean I walked around talking randomly about pots. I actually taught on some verses from the book of Judges—chapter 7, verses 16-22 to be exact. What's happening in these verses is this: God told Gideon, who was the leader of the Israelites, how to beat their enemies, the Midianites. Every one of Gideon's men was supposed to take a horn, a torch, and a pot into battle. They were supposed to keep their torches hidden in pots until Gideon gave the word. So they did. And when Gideon gave them the sign, they smashed their pots, shone their lights, blew their horns, and all shouted like crazy. This scared the Midianites senseless. They started fighting each other instead of the Israelites. So Gideon's army won without really even having to fight. Pretty cool, huh?

This story got me thinking about how we all have torches and pots in our lives. At camp we said the torch is the unique, independent, aware, wonderful person God made each one of us to be. But what do we do? We hide our torches. Because we're afraid we're not skinny and funny enough—or cute and athletic or artistic or smart or...you fill in the blank. We think our torches aren't good enough. If everyone else really saw our torches, they wouldn't like them. And so we hide the torches in pots of all sizes and shapes and colors.

One of your pots might be "trying to do everything right"— if you don't make any mistakes or fail or disappoint anyone, everyone will keep liking you. Your pot might be "looking tough," like nothing ever bothers you. You act sarcastic and make fun of other people. Or your pot might be "flirting with guys," thinking at least you can make them like you, even if no one else does. Maybe your pot even changes with whoever you're around, and you're sweet and smart with some girls, then cool and sarcastic, then athletic. You'll do anything—or be anyone—to be liked.

The Bible would say these pots are sins—which is really just us trying to get our own way apart from God. So one night during the seventh-and-eighth-grade camp we smashed pots. We had a stack of pots sitting in front of the room. And one by one, each person came up, said what her pot was, then walked out in the driveway, threw it down, and smashed it into little bits. The next night each person came back up to the front of the room. Now that our pots were smashed, we could see each other's torches more clearly. As each girl stood in front, all of the other campers told her how they saw God's light in her. They told her she was uniquely and wonderfully made to show God's love to the world.

When you were nine years old, this section wouldn't have made any sense to you at all. But now you're different. You're aware of how the people around you mess up, and you're starting to be aware of how often you do, too. You notice when you accidentally blurt out something that hurts one of your friend's feelings (and you know sometimes you do it on purpose). You say something you shouldn't to your parents. You're mean to your brother; you won't talk to your sister. At Daystar, our counseling ministry, we call this being a mess. The Bible calls it being a sinner.

We've all got pots needing to be smashed. We all need a Savior who will come and smash our pots, forgive us, and help us shine our torches. God loves you. God delights in you. God wants you to be free from the pressure to hide your torch in a pot. It's pretty amazing, when you think about it. Once your pot is smashed, your real light—your independent, unique, beautiful light—can shine.

The Teapot

And now for the part you've been waiting for. This tempest—this stressful, messy, hurtful, confusing time—is all contained in a teapot. If you've never heard the saying "a tempest in a teapot," here's what it means: All of this commotion, this storm that feels so big, is really so small it can fit in a teapot. In other words, it's going to be over soon. You already know most girls say seventh and eighth grades were the hardest times they ever went through. But seventh and eighth grades end. And you go on to become a wonderful, messy, unique, amazing 15-year-old.

5

Mile Marker Five:
MUSCLE MEMORY (15 TO 19)

We didn't train for our 400-mile bike ride. Athletes would have. Most people with brains would have. But we didn't. We laughed (and I, Sissy, cried), saying we were training along the way. That meant each day got a little easier. We took breaks a little less often. And we were a little less tired at the end of each day—which was still really tired, by the way.

The reason for all of these glorious changes? We were developing something called muscle memory. Our muscles were getting used to our putting them through ridiculous amounts of strain, and they were adjusting. (We know it sounds like we're making it up, but it is scientific!) Muscle memory is what makes you brush your teeth in the same way every morning and night (check tonight and you'll see). It's what causes you to brush your hair the same way—or put on your pants or tie your shoes the same way. Your muscles learn through doing something challenging over and over (brushing your teeth was actually new and challenging once upon a time), and then it comes easily. We didn't have to concentrate nearly as much on our last few days of biking, and neither do you as you brush your teeth. You do it without having to try so hard.

You'll develop a good amount of emotional "muscle memory" in the stormy years between 11 and 14. And then you'll get to rest. Your brain will slow down. Relationships will come easier. You'll be more confident in yourself. You'll know more of who you are and what you believe. You'll settle into the person God made you to be. You'll still have uphills, but—just like on our bike ride—you'll be prepared for those uphills in a way you weren't before. And you'll be able to throw your hands up and relax on the long, fun downhills to come.

The Uphills
Body image

Cathy came to Daystar several years ago to help with our summer camps. She was beautiful, a star tennis player, really smart, could sing and play the piano, and had a cute boyfriend and a strong faith. What more could you want, right? Well, one day Cathy had a bad day. She got a rare bad grade on a test, had a fight with her boyfriend, and her car wouldn't start in the parking lot. She sat in her car, all by herself, and screamed. She screamed everything she could think of that she didn't like about herself: "I'm selfish. I can't do anything right. I'm dumb. I always have to be the one who knows the answer," and on and on until she was exhausted. Finally, she ended her screaming fit with, "And I hate my legs!"

That's true for most of us. It might not be our legs we hate. It might be our nose or our hair or our smile or our size. When we've had a bad day, we hate those things even more. We feel this way for two reasons: 1) We think supermodels are real; and 2) our bodies are the bad guys.

First the supermodel dilemma. Most girls secretly wish they could look like supermodels: Long legs, no body fat, nine feet tall—okay, maybe not nine feet, but definitely taller than five feet. We want what we believe—and what the world has taught us—is a perfect body.

We have good news and bad news. The bad news (remember, we like that first) is, it isn't even possible to have that body. Even the women who seem to have those bodies in the pictures you see don't have those bodies in real life. They're computer generated. Computers can take a person's picture and manipulate it and stretch it until she looks more like a green bean than a woman—straight and unbelievably skinny. The good news is, the world is wrong.

The kind of body those pictures think is perfect—the kind you might think is perfect, too—isn't perfect. It hasn't even gone through puberty yet. After you go through puberty, your body is different than it was when you were little. It has more curves—everywhere. God designed it this way so you could have children one day. Bodies that look as if they haven't gone through puberty, that lack those important curves, often don't work right. Girls who are too thin stop or never start their periods, which keeps them in a constant state of puberty/hormone wackiness because their hormones can't get situated. God meant our bodies to have some fat on them—no matter how much the TV, magazines, or even your friends tell you differently.

Now that's out of the way—let's talk about your body as the bad guy. Cathy, from the story earlier, didn't really hate her legs. She didn't love them, like many of us don't love our handwriting or the way we sometimes smile in pictures. But her legs became the enemy. It was easier to be angry at her legs than at all the other things she didn't like about herself, the more painful and out-of-her-control things—like how she treated people or even how other people treated her.

It's pretty easy to let your body take the blame for your problems. But this is where awareness comes in again. When you feel bad about your body, take a minute to think about what's really bothering you. If you notice you eat every time someone hurts your feelings, you're making your body the bad guy rather than the person who hurt you. If you're not eating every time you have dance class, maybe someone at dance class intimidates you. Talk to your mom or a friend or even go see a counselor to figure out whether you dislike something more than just your body. If so, then that's what you need to figure out. Pray for God to help you with the things that are really hurting you, not your very normal and bigger-than-a-supermodel thighs.

What we want you to hear through all of this is: You are beautiful the way you are—no matter what. You have strengths and abilities, gifts and beauty God placed inside you regardless of your size. And we hope you have other people around you who are telling you the same thing. If you're truly unhappy with your body and want to do something about it, talk to your parents or another adult you trust. Ask him to help you find healthy ways to get your body to a weight and shape that helps you feel better about yourself.

Alice came to Daystar several years ago struggling with an eating disorder. She was overweight and throwing up. That summer she helped with our summer camps and ended up talking to a younger girl who was struggling with an eating disorder, too. At the end of the summer Alice told us, "I never knew God could use even this to help someone else."

He can and does. Alice's size didn't matter to God or to the girl she helped. God delights in you and can use you to love and make a difference, no matter what you look like. That's one of the real keys to feeling good about yourself—knowing you're making a difference in the life of someone else.

Peer pressure

If you haven't already been hit by some kind of peer pressure, you will be. And it won't necessarily look like your friends telling you to take drugs or drink alcohol or a boy pushing you to go further physically than you want to. Peer pressure can happen even when no one says a word.

A lot of hidden peer pressure is around you. Whenever other people make it look as if drinking or drugs or sex is fun and no big deal, they send a message that anyone who isn't doing all of that is missing out. But we know so many girls who've believed that lie and ended up miserable. They know the truth—you wake up the next morning feeling much worse than you did before you got drunk or high or messed around with your boyfriend. They know when their parents find out, winning back their trust is one of the biggest uphills a girl can climb.

The girls we talk to tell us how hard it is to deal with all the pressure they face as teenagers. School is hard. Friends can be fickle. You have to keep up in sports and do well in school. You want to belong. And there's a whole lot more. It's no wonder so many girls end up doing things they regret. Here's what one friend of ours told us:

Finding out who you are is a huge part of being a teenager. When I was starting high school, I got caught up in that and headed in the wrong direction. I was starting to find out people can let you down, so I wanted to ease the pain. I wanted to find something that wouldn't let me down, something that would make me feel good, make me not think about the feeling of being sad or upset or let down. I started using drugs and drinking and quickly found out it made me not feel at all. I was the person who made things look fun and easy, but inside I was really falling apart. I got lost trying to walk down the path of figuring out who I was. I found myself being something very far from what I knew I could be or ever wanted to be. I know the Lord has molded and made me, taught me from where I have been. But I will tell you, I still haven't found out who I am—because the Lord teaches me new mercies every morning, and I am forever growing and changing in him. So when I was using drugs and leading a lifestyle that was so gross, I wasn't living in a fun or happy way—it was full of pain. I wasn't living in the way God wanted me to live. I was running from him. It's important to realize the gifts and beauty God has placed inside of you because he has made you each in a way that is unique. You are strong enough to make decisions on your own—and decisions that are the right ones God calls you to.—Mary Ann, 19

Making a difference to someone else is a way to feel good about yourself. And giving in to the pressure to do things you know are wrong is a quick way to feel bad. What typically happens is you do something the first time and feel disappointed in yourself. You get in the situation the next time, think it looks fun, forget all about the disappointment, and do it again. Then you feel even worse. You don't want to feel bad or guilty. So you start doing it over and over as a way to escape the guilt. And then you have an even more serious problem on your hands—something counselors call an addiction.

Peer pressure is an uphill that starts off pretty easy, but gets steeper and steeper the higher you climb. So make sure you've got a group of friends who are making good choices and even pressuring you in a positive way by encouraging you to work for your goals, be yourself, and do what's right. Work hard to make those friendships last during the stormy years so you can enjoy this stage together. A life with no lies or guilt is a whole lot more fun than a life filled with regrets.

Decisions, decisions

When I (Sissy) was 15, I decided to go to a school I didn't want to go to because I didn't want to disappoint my best friend. I got there and hated it and transferred a year later. I (Melissa) didn't make a lot of decisions based on what my friends thought when I was younger. I was the one who talked others into going along with what I wanted. It wasn't good for them—or me. Most of the time it would backfire because they ended up doing something they didn't really want to do.

A lot of big decisions will come your way in the years between 15 and 19—what you want to do after high school, what kind of job you want, who you want to be friends with, who you want to date, if you want to date, what you believe—dealing with who you want to be. And you thought peer pressure sounded bad.

You will have to make tough decisions. They might be tough because you have so many choices. They might be tough because the choices you have aren't necessarily the ones you want. Or they might even be tough because of friends or family who want you to choose one way or another.

This is where all the discovery work you do when you're 13 and 14 will come in handy. Making these decisions will be a lot easier if you have some idea of who you are and who God made you to be. If you have some ideas about that (of course you won't have it all figured out), you can make decisions based on your gifts and talents and passions and hopes instead of what your friends or family or boyfriend think you should do. And don't make decisions for others. Have your own voice and let other people have theirs. And pray—a lot. Ask God to lead you as you make decisions.

In the Old Testament book of Numbers we find the story of the Israelites getting ready to take possession of the Promised Land (someone else was already there). But first they had to check it out. So they sent in spies to see if they had any chance of taking over. Twelve spies went into Canaan (the name of this land) and came back talking about how amazing the land was. They also talked about giants. "They said, 'The land we explored devours those living in it. All of the people we saw there are of great size...We seemed like grasshoppers in our own eyes and we looked the same to them'" (Numbers 13:32-33).

These men tried to convince everyone not to go. They were trying to make decisions for the others. But two of the spies—Caleb and Joshua—disagreed with the rest. They stood up to the other 10 men and made their own decisions based on who they were and what they believed God wanted.

God's response was pretty clear. He basically told all the other spies they wouldn't see the Promised Land. But Caleb and Joshua would because they followed God. God said, "But because my servant Caleb has a different spirit and follows me wholeheartedly, I will bring him into the land he went to, and his descendants will inherit it" (Numbers 14:24).

Some of the decisions you will face in your high school years may make you feel as small and insignificant as a grasshopper. But you can have a different spirit, like Caleb. As you seek God's guidance in your decisions and go where you feel God leading you, God will bring you into a land more amazing than you can imagine.

How do you find that land, you might be wondering? How do you know where God is leading you? Like we've said before, listen. Listen to your heart. Allow yourself to be thirsty and pay attention to what quenches your thirst. Notice what you enjoy the most and what makes you feel the most like yourself. Listen to your parents and teachers, your friends (ones you trust), coaches, and mentors. God can and does speak through the people in our lives.

Think About It

Take a minute to write about some of the things or people in your life that make you feel like an insignificant grasshopper.

How could God be calling you to have a different spirit, like Caleb?

Where do you think God might be speaking to you, and what do you think God is saying?

The Downhills
The end of hiccups

Hiccups have to be one of the most annoying little problems you can have. You can't talk, you can't be quiet, and you can't think about anything else...which just keeps the hiccups coming. My (Sissy's) grandfather, who was a doctor, told me something inside of you gets flipped upside down, and as you relax and think about something else, it flips back over. I don't know how true that really is, but it kind of makes sense. How many times have you had the hiccups, and then all of a sudden, they're gone. They seem to disappear as mysteriously as they appear.

The hiccups in confidence you experience in the pre-stormy and stormy years come and go just as mysteriously. Somewhere between 15 and 19, those hiccups pretty much go away. You're finally free to think about all kinds of things besides what other people think of you.

Last spring we met with a group of high school girls. We started talking about their parents and what growing up was like for their parents. As each girl talked about her mom or dad, she realized something. One of the girls put it this way: "I never realized how many of our parents had such hard lives."

These girls had heard their parents tell the same stories for years. But until now their hiccups in confidence kept them from really seeing what their parents' lives were like. It was as if their own worries and thoughts and self-consciousness only allowed them to see themselves (and maybe their closest friends).

As the hiccups in confidence come to an end, the self-consciousness lifts. You will always have those times when you feel insecure or worry about what others think. But once you get through the stormy years, you start to see and love and understand with fewer fears—and fewer hiccups.

Idealism

When I was 16, I (Melissa) had just gotten involved with my high school youth group. I don't really remember what I was doing before, but it wasn't going to youth group. I finally caught on and joined. And I loved it. We talked about our faith and sang songs and loved being together. But we had one problem. We didn't have a youth director. So I decided to do something about it. I made an appointment to talk to my minister.

I marched into Dr. Childs' office and told him our problem.

"Dr. Childs," I told him, "things are going great right now with the youth group, but we really need a youth director. I just wanted you to know that, until you can find one, I would be happy to step in."

> *I wish I had known when your parents say you can't do something or go somewhere or shouldn't watch or listen to certain things, etc.—it's not because they want to make your life miserable. It's because they're looking out for you and want what's best for you.*
> *—Betsy, 19*

And I did. At 16 I became the youth director of my church. I hadn't been a Christian very long, and I didn't know much about Scripture. (Sounds a little like our 400-mile bike ride, doesn't it?) But I had one thing as a 16-year-old that is a huge downhill for this age: I was idealistic.

Idealism is the belief you can do just about anything and it will turn out great. You probably don't have a lot of idealism right now—too many hiccups and hormones are in your way. You might have lots of great ideas, but you probably keep a lot of them to yourself because you don't want to sound dumb. Or you don't want to disappoint anyone if things don't turn out the way you planned. But in the years after the storm, as your confidence returns, your idealism will come back with it. Together they make just the right combination to let go of those worries about what everyone else thinks and go for it.

Purpose

If there was one word you'd want other people to use to describe you, what would it be? We asked girls from 11 to 19 years old that same question. These are their answers:

11-to-14-year-olds	15-to-19-year-olds
cool	strong-willed (but not in a bad way)
fun to be around	
smart	stand up for what I believe
funny	respected
considerate	loving
caring	original
perfect	shining the light of the Lord
popular	unique
trustworthy	loyal
not bad (not in trouble)	selfless
hip	pure-hearted
a best friend	beautiful (not just in looks)
sunshine	magnetic
	deep and perceptive

Both groups have some great words. They all sound pretty attractive. But can you tell a difference? Most of the words for the 11-to-14-year-olds have to do with what other people think of them. But 15-to-19-year-olds are starting to think about something different. They're thinking about who they want to be inside, what their characters will be. They're thinking about what they want out of life—and what they want to offer to the people they love and to the world in general. They know life is about a lot more than what they thought it was in middle school. Now they want to make a difference, to know their lives have a deeper purpose.

We do a certain personality test with many of the girls who come to Daystar. To figure out which personality you are, you answer yes or no to a lot of different statements. One of those is, "I want to make the world a better place." Often, 11-to-14-year-olds read that statement and say, "Not really." Sometimes it's because they don't believe they can make a difference. They don't believe they're smart enough or popular enough or any of the words in the 11-to-14-year-old column above to make a difference, so why try? Sometimes it's because they're so caught up in themselves, they don't really care. Those girls often come to feel differently as they get older.

Even if you don't feel like you are those things listed in either column, you can make a difference. All you have to do is care about someone else—because that's how purpose starts. If you can help one person by smiling at her or being kind in some little way, you've made a difference. Like so many things, purpose brings more purpose. Once you've made a difference, you'll just want to do more. And that's when you'll finally start to believe you matter.

Several years ago I (Sissy) got a call from a man who told me his daughter wanted him to take all the money he would've used on her Christmas gifts and give it to Daystar. We know! It's hard for us to believe, too. A lot of kids who come to counseling and camps with Daystar can't afford it on their own, so other kind people give money to help them. This girl (her name was Lisa) wanted to be one of those people.

The next week I had breakfast with Lisa. Before we get to what she said, let me give you the back-story. Lisa came to Daystar very depressed. She dressed in all black. Her hair hung in her face. And she had actually even tried to hurt herself. So her parents brought her to Daystar.

Over the next few months, Lisa started to look and act very different. She held her head a little higher. She smiled more and talked to the other girls. She started to have hope again, believing her life mattered.

Now back to breakfast. Lisa told me Daystar had made a huge impact on her life. And what made the most impact was something one of the other girls had said to her. Lisa said, "I remember we were at a group meeting a few weeks after I started doing better. Ashley [a girl who was really struggling at the time] was talking about how hard things were. Then she turned and looked directly at me. She said, 'Lisa, you are a bridge of hope to me. When you came in, you felt like I do on my very worst days. But you're different now. And you make me want to be different, too. It's like you're showing me who I can be.'" In that one comment Lisa knew she'd made a difference in Ashley's life. She knew her life had a purpose.

Girls crave this kind of purpose, especially in the years between ages 15 and 19. Even now you might read Lisa's story and think, "I want to make that kind of difference." You can. You can make a difference to your friends and to your parents. You can make a difference to younger children or people in your community or in other parts of the world who need help. Thinking about others is a great way to stop thinking about yourself—and that imaginary audience you believe is watching you.

You don't have to be defined by the hard parts of growing up. You can choose to have a different spirit, like Caleb. Find places to volunteer with younger kids. Talk to your friends when they're sad. Do something nice for your mom or dad or grandmother or sibling. You will have giants in your life—mean friends, body issues, parent struggles. But you can rise above all of it and be the girl of tremendous purpose God made you to be. We promise you'll feel a whole lot better about yourself if you do.

You have much to look forward to in the years to come. Life gets easier in a lot of ways. But you have so much to look forward to right now. God is making you into a young woman with depth and purpose and hope—and you can start to discover now just how fun and freeing it is to go ahead and be you.

Part Two

WHAT DO I WANT MOST IN MY LIFE?

6

Did you ever read *Anne of Green Gables* as a little girl? It's the story of a girl named Anne Shirley who moves in with a sister and brother named Marilla and Matthew Cuthbert. Anne is pretty close to your age and probably a lot like you. She loves adventures. She gets in trouble from time to time, although she very rarely means to. And the very most important thing in her life is her best friend, Diana.

Before she meets Diana, Anne is desperate for friendship, for a connection to someone she can laugh with and play with and talk with until all hours of the night. In a conversation with Marilla, Anne talks about how much she wants a friend and goes on to describe that friend like this: "An intimate friend, you know—a really kindred spirit to whom I can confide my inmost soul. I've dreamed of meeting her all my life. I never really supposed I would, but so many of my loveliest dreams have come true all at once that perhaps this one will, too." (Montgomery, 57)

Can you relate to Anne's words? To what she wants? We sure can. As girls we want connection. We want friendship and closeness and to share all the things we love with someone—or many someones—who are important to us. We want to be liked and loved. And we want it desperately. This longing for close friends is a significant part of how God designed us as girls.

Girls and Boys: The Difference

Have you ever been to a school dance? If not, you have a lot to look forward to. Dances are fun—and funny. We both loved them when we were growing up. There's usually good music. Sometimes there's food and punch. But the best part is hanging out with your friends. And boys. The boys are kind of the funny part—especially in middle school.

At middle school dances, girls and boys are typically doing—and thinking—completely different things. Here's the scene: Picture your school gym, only a little more colorful, with balloons and streamers. The chaperones (teachers and parents) are wandering through the crowd, checking to make sure no one is getting into trouble, and whispering to each other about who might. The DJ is at the front of the room running the music and lights and watching over a mostly empty dance floor. The guys and the girls, rather than dancing, are standing on opposite sides of the gym. The boys are pushing and throwing ice at each other—playing around. The girls are standing in clumps. They dance a little—in a clump. Then they get punch or food—in a clump. And then they go to the bathroom—in the very same clump.

What are all these nondancing guys and clumped-up girls thinking? Well, the guys are thinking, *I don't want to look like a fool. I'm afraid to walk across the gym floor to ask that girl to dance. I'm going to try to look like I don't care.* So they throw ice rather than look like fools. Hmmm.

The girls—all the way on the other side of the room—are thinking, *Is he looking at me? Is that boy ever going to come over here and ask me to dance?* Or, *Pleeeeeaaaase don't let anyone come over here and ask me to dance!* Not exactly like *High School Musical*, is it? But believe it or not, the boys have a reason for what they're doing, and the girls have a reason for what they're doing.

Let's talk about the boys first. As you know, God made girls and guys very different. Not only do we look different, but also our brains and emotions are completely different. That makes us want different things.

Psychologists have actually studied the ways men and women are different. They talk about how men and women—and therefore boys and girls—find happiness and fulfillment (feeling good about who we are and what we do) in different ways. It turns out men find their fulfillment in feeling as if they matter and in being independent. Women find their fulfillment in caring for others and being *inter*dependent. In other words, men (and boys) want to feel like they are important and can be important by themselves. They don't want to feel like they always need someone else to do things for them. Women (and girls) want to be connected to other people. We like to do things together (that's what the prefix "inter" means—together). We like to care about each other and have others care about us.

Don't get us wrong. Boys want relationships, too. They want to have friends and be loved. But that's not what makes them feel the very best about themselves. And girls want to have purpose. We want to feel like we're important and can accomplish things, but often we want to do those things for someone else or know we're important in the eyes of someone who matters to us. We want a shared purpose.

Now back to the dance. The boys don't want to look like fools because a fool is the opposite of someone important. They want to feel as if they can walk across the dance floor and ask a girl to dance. But she might say no. And then they wouldn't look very important. So it's easier never to walk across the floor in the first place than to risk not looking important.

What about the girls in their clumps? Clumps are basically our way of knowing we're connected and someone cares about us. Our relationships with the boys are a little riskier. We want to be asked to dance, to be chosen. But they might not choose us. So we stay in our clumps where we feel safe and cared about.

Girls long for relationships. We want to matter to someone else and have others matter to us. We want friends. We want to be close to our moms, dads, or grandparents (or if that's hard to admit, you can at least admit you want them to love you and think you're great). We might even want to be chosen by boys. We want to be known and liked and loved. It is one of the most important parts of how God made us. Because of our wants, our relationships have the power to make us feel great about ourselves—or make us feel pretty terrible.

The Hard Part

What would you say is the hardest part of being a girl? Take a minute to write down two or three answers.

We took a survey of girls between seven and 18 years old. This is what they said:

7-to-9-year-olds	• Other people laughing at me • Picking out clothes • Being teased by boys • Being left out • Parents yelling at you
10-to-11-year-olds	• Crying • Shaving, dealing with periods, doing hair • Being bullied and yelled at in school • Trying not to gossip • Keeping up with homework
12-to-14-year-olds	• Dealing with gossip and critical girls • Having to get the right kind of clothes • Having to be someone you're not to fit in • Worrying about peer pressure and what other people think about you • Worrying about impressing guys • Dealing with emotions (especially during your period)
15-to-16-year-olds	• Trying to fit in • Worrying about how you look • Getting caught in the middle of drama with other girls—fights, competition, overanalyzing things, gossip • Not knowing if you can trust a guy • Dealing with periods and maturing faster or slower than your friends
17-to-19-year-olds	• Feeling like you have to look good because you're a girl • Dealing with how cruel girls are to each other • Dealing with popularity (or lack of it) and self-esteem (or lack of it) • Thinking boys will make us happy and then seeing how immature they are at our age • Dealing with emotions, especially around your period

What do you notice about these girls' answers? Are any of yours the same? We would guess so. Ours are, too—and probably your mom's, your grandmothers', your aunts'. (Why don't you go ask them?) Clearly, being a girl has its challenges all along the way.

If we were to do a pie chart (which we won't because we don't want you to feel like you're in school—and we don't have a clue how to do them anymore), periods would get a little slice of the pie. Appearance would get a slice that's just a bit bigger. But the biggest piece, the one that would make up almost the whole pie, would be relationships. It could be relationships with boys, friends, or family—it doesn't matter. Relationships seem to give us girls quite a bit of trouble.

The real question is why relationships are so hard when they're something God made us for. Well, you can probably answer that question better than we can because you know how it feels to have a best friend who makes friends with someone else, and then the two of them leave you out. You know how it feels when your friends have a sleepover and don't call you. You know how it feels when your older brother embarrasses you in front of your friends. You know how it feels when the boy you think is cute makes fun of you in front of his friends. You know how it feels when your parents fight. And you know how it feels when you hurt someone you care about.

All of that—and there can be so much more—feels cruddy, to say the least. Relationships can be hard for one primary reason—the messy part of us called sin.

You might already know the story of how sin started with Adam and Eve. If you don't, here are the highlights: Adam and Eve were living in a place called the Garden of Eden. They were the first two people ever to live, well, anywhere.

God gave them everything they could ever want—animals to name, all kinds of great food to eat. They didn't have to work. They could just hang out with each other and their animal friends and do anything they wanted to do—well, almost anything. God told them not to eat the fruit from one particular tree in the garden. So what do you think Adam and Eve did? They did the same thing you want to do when someone says you can do anything you want *except* _____. You want to do whatever you just filled in the blank with. And that's what Adam and Eve did. They ate the apple. From then on things were different. That choice, sometimes called "the fall," is when sin came into the world. And sin is still a part—a strong part—of all of us. (You can read more about sin in the Bible. Check out Genesis 2 and 3 and Romans 3:22-23.)

Every time you say something hurtful to a friend, every time you are disrespectful to your parents, lie, take something that isn't yours, gossip about a girl at school, or do something you know you shouldn't have done, you're feeling the effects of the fall.

We're all sinners, which means all of our friends (girls and boys) and parents and grandparents and everyone else we have relationships with are, too. So we hurt their feelings. They hurt ours. We leave someone out. We get left out. And on and on.

Think about all of your relationships for a minute. You probably can't think of one that hasn't disappointed you—even just a little bit. We are all imperfect, so our relationships are, too. And this is what makes relationships hard.

When Elizabeth was in eighth grade, she had a lot of struggles with friends. She was part of a group of girls who were fun and kind to her. They were a little boy crazy, and honestly, she was probably more mature than they were. But they were good friends.

Eventually, Elizabeth got tired of the boy craziness. She forgot what she liked in these friends and only saw the bad in them. Another group of girls was much more popular—and Elizabeth wanted to be. So she started pulling away from the first group. She stopped sitting with them at lunch and instead tried to find a spot at the popular girls' table. When her old friends would ask her to spend the night the next weekend, she would make them wait for her answer, hoping one of the popular girls would invite her over instead.

Can you guess what happened to Elizabeth? Her old friends figured out what was going on. They realized she didn't really want to be with them, so they quit asking. But Elizabeth finally got what she wanted. The popular girls slowly started to include her. In the beginning it was thrilling. She felt more important walking down the hall just because she was walking with them. She was included in their parties and had a regular seat at their lunch table.

A few months later things changed. The more she hung out with these girls, the more she realized they weren't really very good friends. They said horrible things behind each other's backs. They were rude to their parents. And they were a whole lot more boy crazy than her old friends. But when she wanted her old friends back, they had moved on. They had new friends and stories and experiences she was no longer part of—something Elizabeth would tell you today was one of the hardest parts of her life as a girl so far.

What's the moral of Elizabeth's story? Elizabeth—like all of us—lives in a fallen world. Her first group of friends wasn't perfect, but they were real friends. So try to remember the people in your life aren't perfect, either. When your friends hurt your feelings, forgive them. You'll all feel better.

Boys will make mistakes. So be understanding and forgiving. At the same time, don't let boys treat you with anything less than the kindness and respect you deserve. Remember, you're wonderful and ought to be treated that way.

The adults in your life will make mistakes, too. They love you a lot, but they will mess up. We'll talk more about this in the next chapter.

But we have good news—really good news. Sometime you will have perfect relationships—when you are with God in heaven. Until then relationships will have their uphills and downhills. You'll have fun times and disappointments. Parents will be loving and kind and then forget something you think is really important. Sometimes relationships will work exactly the way we hoped they would, and sometimes they'll seem broken beyond repair. Until we're in heaven, our need for perfect relationships will only be fulfilled in short spurts.

That doesn't mean you'll never find good, meaningful relationships. God made you to deeply want relationships, to love and be loved by other people. And God wouldn't have done that if it wasn't possible to have right here on earth. So you can hope for and expect good things in your relationships. You can have friends who are fun and kind and even challenge you when they see you hurt someone else. God can and will give you all kinds of relationships to bring out the best in you.

The best part of all this is even though our relationships with people will always be a little disappointing, one relationship never will be—the one you have with God. And as much as you want to be loved and enjoyed by your parents, friends, and even boys, your desire for a relationship with God goes deeper still.

Think About It

Write about a time when a relationship has disappointed you. How did that situation get resolved?

Have there been times when you've disappointed your friends? Why is it hard to accept that we all disappoint others sometimes?

The Deepest Desire

I (Sissy) heard about Jesus for the first time when I was 12. Actually, I'd heard about him before at church, but I hadn't paid a whole lot of attention. Then I went to camp. I was at that thirsty, stormy age and must have been ready for things to change. Because they did.

I don't remember a lot about that week. I know we sang fun songs and played games, and I made some new friends. And I actually started my period—which was *not* the best time to start my period. But the most vivid memory I have is this:

I was walking by myself across the barn floor. We must have just heard someone talk about the cross because it was all I could think about. And I remember thinking, *This is unbelievable. If everyone knew this, they would be so happy.*

What I knew was Jesus loved me. I knew he not only loved me but also thought I was wonderful and smart and beautiful and brilliant and delightful. He wanted to be my best friend. And he was a friend I could always talk to. He would never let me down or hurt me. He wanted to take care of me and protect me and give me really good things in life, like friends and people who loved me. And he wanted those things so much, he died on the cross. He did that for me. He did that so sin wouldn't have control of me or my life. He did that so good could win. Jesus died on the cross so I could have hope in the midst of girls who hurt my feelings and my own desire to do things I wasn't supposed to do. He was bigger than that, and now he was alive in my heart so I could be bigger than those things, too.

That summer everything changed for me. God became a part of my life—the most important part. He became my best friend. Twenty-six years later, he is still the only friend I've ever had who hasn't disappointed me. And I've had some pretty great friends. But Jesus is one who always loves me, always delights in me, and always wants to know the deepest parts of my heart. And he feels the very same way about you. Jesus says, "I no longer call you servants, because servants do not know their master's business. Instead, I have called you friends, for everything that I learned from my Father I have made known to you" (John 15:15).

You can read more about it in the Bible, especially in Romans 5:8; Ephesians 3:14-21; and Romans 8:28-39. If you discover something in those verses that's confusing to you or makes you want to know more, talk to you parents or a friend who goes to church or someone else you trust. Ask them to help you learn more about Jesus and the tremendous love he has for you.

7

Mile Marker Seven:
FAMILY SECRETS

Between the two of us we've worked with more than 10,000 families over the years. We have had more than 10,000 kids tell us what they struggle with and worry about—a lot of it having to do with their families.

You might have a great relationship with your family or one you wish were a little different. You might get frustrated with your dad or hurt by your mom. Your little brother might wander into your room, or your sister might borrow your clothes without asking. This chapter is about those things. It contains a few of the secrets we've discovered in our talks with kids and families, secrets to help make hard—or even good—relationships with your family better.

Moms

God gave you your mom. Whether she gave birth to you, adopted you, or became like a mom to you when she married your dad, God had a reason to put you and this person together. Maybe you can tell exactly what that is, or maybe you have no idea and are wondering what God was thinking. Either way, we want you to know a lot more about moms.

Secret #1: Your mom will not be like any other mom.
You might have friends whose moms seem really great. When

95

you're at their houses, these moms are fun and cool and really easy to talk to. They don't seem anything like your mom. And that's why you like them—they aren't your mom. But ask the friend whose mom you're thinking of how she feels about her

mom. She probably feels a lot like you feel about your own mom. That "fun" mom has to wake her kids up even when they don't want to wake up. She tells her teenagers no when they want to go to the mall with their friends. She gets frustrated when your friend makes bad grades.

Some moms don't give consequences or rules at all. You may go through times in your life when you would really like to have one of those moms. But we have counseled a lot of girls who do. And they wish their moms were different.

Several years ago a girl in high school said to me (Melissa), "I wish my mom would ground me. I never get in trouble for anything, and I've even started trying to do things that would make her give me consequences. It's almost like she doesn't notice or care enough to stop me." Girls whose parents never give them any kinds of rules often feel this way about their parents. They don't feel safe or as if their parents care about them. When you have a mom who expects the best from you, it is because she believes you're capable of it. And even when you'd like to trade her in, that's a pretty great kind of mom to have.

Secret #2: Your mom is smarter than you think she is.

There's a funny saying that when we're young, our parents seem really smart. When we're teenagers, our parents turn kind of dumb, and when we're adults, our parents suddenly get really smart again. Why do you think this is? The intelligence level of our parents doesn't change when we're teenagers. We just think it does.

This is especially true with moms. When you were little, you thought your mom was the smartest person in the universe. You asked her a million questions: "Mommy, why do dogs have tails?" "Mommy, why is the grass green?" And so on. You asked her because you absolutely believed she knew the answers. But then you hit these pre-stormy and stormy years. And we would guess you stopped asking.

Part of the reason you don't ask is because you're trying to figure things out for yourself. You want to have your own opinions and thoughts and ideas. And your mom usually tells you hers. She does this because you used to want to know. And you probably didn't wake up one day and say, "Mom, I'd really like to decide things for myself now. Would you mind not telling me things so often and letting me try to figure them out first?" Or if you have said that, we would guess you said it with what she would call a "tone."

Your mom is still really smart. She can give you her opinion, and you can still decide for yourself. Sometimes it helps to know what other people think, then use their thoughts to help you form your own ideas. It also helps to talk to your mom instead of just deciding you don't need her opinion now that you're older. Let her know—nicely—it's not that you don't care what she thinks. It's that you're trying to figure things out for yourself. Try to be patient with her while you're figuring those things out. It can be sad for moms to watch their little girls grow up.

Believe it or not, your mom probably went through a lot of what you're going through right now. She was a teenager with some of the same thoughts and feelings you have. Now she has the advantage of living a few more years, which gives her a lot more wisdom. Asking for your mom's help or advice doesn't make you immature or stupid. It's actually a pretty smart way to gain some wisdom of your own.

Secret #3: You can be a teenager and be kind to your mom at the same time.

It seems like the normal thing for teenage girls to be rude to their moms. Do you remember the scene in *Freaky Friday* where Lindsay Lohan screams at her mom, "You're ruining my life!" That's the kind of thing teenagers in movies say to their moms. A lot of real-life teenagers say the same thing.

So many of the girls we know live in a constant state of irritation with their moms. Again, this is because they're trying to figure out who they are—separate from their moms. So rather than knowing that and just being okay with who their moms are, most teenagers get critical, rolling their eyes and arguing with every little thing their moms say. The girls stomp upstairs and slam doors (until their doors get taken off the hinges) and call their friends to say how ridiculous their moms are acting.

Most of the time when a girl feels as if her mom is ruining her life, it's because her mom is trying to protect her. When your mom says you can't do something you really want to do, she might be trying to keep you from making a bad decision; she might be trying to protect you from people or places she knows could be dangerous for you. She might be trying to guide you toward making better choices down the road. Believe it or not, your mom doesn't want you to be grounded or punished. She wants you to be safe, to be secure, to be all the wonderful things she knows you can be.

When your mom gives you a consequence or tells you no and you talk back to her, you feel bad about it later. Then because you feel bad, you don't really want to be around her. This makes her more hurt and frustrated with you. Then you get even more frustrated with her. It just keeps getting worse and worse.

Sometimes girls are mean to their moms because deep inside they're afraid of being independent. So they think if they can get mad enough—or make their moms mad enough—it won't be so hard to grow up and not need their moms anymore. But this, too, just makes the mother-daughter relationship harder than it has to be. If you feel this way, try to remember nothing's wrong with needing your mom. Every grown woman still needs her mom now and then.

You don't have to be the screaming, smoldering, disrespectful teenage girl from the movies. And we know you don't really want to be. Maybe you can write your mom a note every once in a while to tell her you love her. Every mom has a special place where she keeps all the pictures and notes her children have made for her. Yours does, too. And because you're becoming your own person, these probably mean even more to her than they ever have. Hug your mom every once in a while. Ask her to watch a movie or TV with you. Invite her to take a walk and actually talk to her, rather than just listening to your iPod. It will help both of you feel a whole lot better about your relationship and about yourselves.

Secret #4: There's a middle ground between telling your mom everything and nothing.

"I feel like my mom wants to know everything about my life. It's like she wants to be my best friend." We hear this so many times from so many girls. Let's set the record straight: Your mom doesn't want to be your best friend. She knows you have best friends your age, and she wants you to have those friends. But she does want to know something about your life because she cares and because she worries.

My (Sissy's) mom says worrying is a mom's number-one job. And that's what moms do. They worry about you when you leave the house, when you're with friends (especially with boys), when you spend the night with someone else, just about any time they're not with you. They honestly can't help themselves.

> I wish I had known my mom really was right about who I should and shouldn't hang out with. It would've saved me from getting hurt many times.—Maggie, 15

If you want your mom to worry a little less, your best bet is to be honest with her. Give her a little information— even before she asks for it—like where you're going, who you're going with, and what time you'll be home. This kind of information helps moms worry a little less.

When your mom picks you up from school or plops down next to you on the couch when she gets home from work, she's not trying to bug you. She's trying to find out how you're doing. She wants to know what's going well and what isn't. She wants to know because she loves you. That's what people do when they care about each other—they talk to each other.

Still, you don't have to tell your mom everything. She probably doesn't even want to know everything because then she might worry more. But you can tell her a little. You can let her in on your life in a way that lets her know she's still important to you and part of your world.

Secret #5: Your mom is not always the bad guy.

When we're at camp, we start every morning with a few questions for the girls. One of these questions is, "Who do you look up to the most?" Almost all of the second through sixth graders say their moms. Almost none of the seventh and eighth graders do. This goes back to the whole thing about wanting to be your own person. So often it feels like your mom is the person who gets in your way the most.

But something else is going on here, too. It's called displacement. Maybe you remember displacement from science class. It's what happens when you put rocks in a pan of water—the water level rises because the rocks push the water out of its place, and the water has to go somewhere else.

In people, emotions get displaced all the time. When a friend hurts your feelings at school, you probably try really hard to keep those hurt feelings inside. You keep going—smiling and trying to act as if nothing's bothering you. But those feelings have to go somewhere. So when you get home, out they come.

Now you probably don't cry to your mom as soon as you see her (although that would actually be helpful). Instead when she asks, "How was your day?" you might say something in a not-so-nice tone like, "I don't want to talk today, Mom." Or maybe you just ignore her and walk away. Then when she asks you to clean up your room or help set the table or pick up your backpack, you come unglued. You get angry.

Your mom is not always the bad guy. Sometimes she has to be because she's trying to protect you (remember that?). But other times she gets blamed for something she had nothing to do with. Your friend hurt your feelings, but you yell at your mom. That's displacement.

Our emotions have to come out somewhere. If we don't let them out in healthy ways—like talking about them or journaling or even painting or drawing—they'll probably come out in not-so-healthy ways. We'll yell at our moms, or we'll cry and act like something she said is the biggest deal in the world when, on another day, we would've been able to just let it go.

If you notice yourself doing this, maybe you could try talking to your mom about what's really going on. She really does want to know. And again you don't have to tell her every detail. But we can assure you: In your mom you have someone who will always love you, always want to know about you, and always want the best for you.

Think About It

This week, make a point of thinking about these secrets in your relationship with your mom. Write down what you've discovered about your mom and your relationship with her.

In the next section, we'll be talking about dads. After you read it, come back and write down how this information changes the way you think about your dad.

Now that you understand them a little better, write down three ideas for improving your relationship with each of your parents.

Dads

We know a lot of girls, especially in divorced homes, who hit their teenage years and stop spending time with their dads. It may be because they're spending most of their time with their friends. It may be because their dads embarrass them, try to teach them too much, or are critical. Dads aren't perfect. But your dad is still your dad. And your dad helps you know God and yourself in ways no one else can. That's why it's worth knowing a little more about why dads are the way they are.

Secret #1: Your dad is just as confused about your relationship as you are.

When you were growing up, you and your dad probably did lots of things together. You played sports. You snuggled up to watch TV. You went hiking or waterskiing or to baseball games. There was no end to the fun the two of you shared— until adolescence hit.

Now you'd rather hang out with your friends than hike with your dad. You'd rather go to the mall than to a baseball game. You don't want to watch the same shows as him—and if you do, you'd rather watch them in the other room.

By now you know these changes have to do with your age. But your dad doesn't. All he knows is, you don't really want to spend time with him anymore. And he's not really sure why. So maybe he's acting a little possessive, which bugs you. Or maybe he's doing the opposite and trying not to bother you, which bugs you. Either way, you need to know he's a little confused by all these changes, too.

Secret #2: You are your dad's best teacher.

I (Melissa) remember the last time I went fishing with my dad. He told me I was too big to go anymore. And I watched him go out in the boat with my little brother. I still wanted to go, but I didn't tell him. And he had no idea.

Your dad sees the outside changes going on with you in these years. He knows you are becoming a woman. But he really doesn't know how he's supposed to connect with you. And he's not sure you want to connect with him.

Help your dad out. I (Sissy) remember my dad teaching me to fish when I was little. As I got older, he taught me to swing dance. I loved it, and I'm pretty sure I would ask him to help me. It was one of my favorite things for us to do together—and I think it was one of his. But he didn't know I liked it until I told him.

Tell your dad the things you like to do with him. Ask him to take you to get coffee or ice cream. Have him teach you to dance—or fish. He wants to be a part of your life but might not know how. You're the best person in the world to tell him.

Secret #3: Dads are grown-up boys.

Remember all those differences between boys and girls? Boys

want to feel like they're important and independent, while girls want to feel connected.

When boys come to Daystar, they talk a whole lot more when they're playing basketball or cards. It's much harder for them to talk when they're just sitting. They're doers. Girls, on the other hand, can sit and talk for hours. We're relaters.

Your dad is a grown-up boy. He probably won't come in and sit on your bed and talk to you for hours like your mom will. But he'll talk to you while you're shooting hoops or playing golf or working in the yard.

Get out and do things with your dad. Kick the soccer ball. Learn to dance. Play tennis. You can be a relater, he can be a doer, and you can enjoy each other a lot while you're at it.

Secret #4: Your dad's goal in life isn't to embarrass you.

Not only are dads doers, but they're also players. By nature dads tend to be silly and fun and playful and don't care very much about what other people think. This, again, is one of those things you loved when you were little. But now that you're this age, it feels totally different. When your dad sings in the car, walks out to get the paper in his bathrobe, or honks and waves to pick you up from school, it's *really* embarrassing. But that's not why he does it. He does it because it's him.

You're trying to figure out who you are and want the freedom to be that person. Your dad wants that same freedom. Let your dad be silly. He does it because he loves you and loves to play with you. And you might be surprised how much you can still enjoy him.

Secret #5: Your dad is an imperfect, important part of your life.

You may have heard people say you'll marry someone a lot like your dad. You may hear this and think, "I hope I get to marry someone like him." Or maybe you think, "No way! I want to marry someone completely opposite of my dad." No matter how you feel about your dad, your relationship with him has a huge impact on who you will date and possibly marry one day. It has a huge impact on how you feel about yourself. Your dad is the first man in your life. He shows you how men are supposed to treat women—what it means to be valued and respected by a guy.

Your dad might do these things really well. We know lots of dads who tell their girls how wonderful and beautiful they are. They spend one-on-one time with their daughters just to get to know them and show them how special they are. If you have a dad like this, you might start to feel awkward about spending time with him as you get older. We encourage you to push through that awkwardness and keep spending time with him. You will learn so much about relationships with the opposite sex through this kind of time and communication with your dad. And in a few years it won't feel awkward any-more. Then you'll be glad you kept building a great relation-ship with your dad.

You might have a dad who doesn't do these things very well. It's not that he doesn't think you're wonderful and beau-tiful and valued—he just doesn't know how to tell you or show you. Guys don't express how they feel in the ways girls do. So talk to your dad. Tell him how you'd like your relation-ship to be. As we said, you're the best teacher he has on the subject of you. If you want to spend more time with him, tell him. If you want more hugs or more laughter or more sup-port, tell him—kindly and gently. If your dad still doesn't get it, you need to remember it's not because there's something wrong with you. Some dads just have a hard time connecting with their daughters because of their own struggles and problems. If you and your dad are having a hard time connecting and you can't seem to get through to him, talk to your mom or another adult you trust. We often counsel girls and dads (and girls and moms) to help them develop better relationships. Sometimes it takes another adult to help parents see how they can build stronger connections with their children. Don't be afraid to ask for help.

No matter which kind of dad you have, your relationship with him is an important part of your life. Spend time with him. Have fun with him. Ask him what he thinks and believes. And then tell him about you. Your dad wants to know—and wants to be connected to you. And you are the best one to help him learn how.

8

Mile Marker Eight:
Even More Family Secrets

I (Melissa) was in the middle of two brothers growing up. I (Sissy) was an only child until I was 16 and then had a baby sister. We had, obviously, very different experiences. And those experiences have a lot to do with who we are today.

We also had all kinds of other people in our lives—some were actual family, some were close enough to feel like family. You have these people, too. And all of these people—siblings, grandparents, aunts and uncles, and close family friends—are important parts of who you are and who you're becoming.

Brothers and Sisters

Papers and books and even whole college classes exist about how the order in which you were born affects your personality. We want to tell you a little about that—only we'll leave out the boring, psychology-ish stuff.

The oldest child

Oldest children are usually children who try very hard to please their parents. They want their parents' approval and can very easily grow up to be perfectionists (they want to do everything right). The oldest child also has Mom and Dad—and all their attention—to himself for a while. Then siblings come along, and the oldest child is forced to share. So he can easily end up resenting the younger pipsqueaks in the family.

If you're an oldest child, you've probably been told your younger brothers and sisters look up to you. Your parents are right. They do. Even when they're being bratty, they're doing it because they want your attention. What you do—what you say to them and the attention you give them—matters. Be careful how you talk to them when you're angry. Your words have a lot of power.

> *Surrounding yourself with a good group of friends (not just one) in high school is very important. And I wish I had known how quickly time goes by.—Megan, 17*

And it doesn't hurt you too much to let them hang out with you every so often. One of these days you'll want to be their friend—and it's a whole lot easier when you've had a good relationship growing up.

The middle child

Most middle children have a hard time feeling like they're as important as their brothers and sisters. They feel the oldest gets lots of attention and, of course, the youngest does. So sometimes they feel lost.

If you're a middle child, we can assure you you're not lost. Remember how we said sometimes your feelings are the result of the changes in your brain, not the actions and words of other people? This definitely applies to how your parents feel about you. You are just as loved as every other member of your family—no matter when you were born.

If you're struggling to figure out your place in your family, try figuring out what your place is in life, rather than just in your family...who you are and what makes you feel the best about yourself. Find something you love and can do that's different from what your siblings do. Pick a different sport. Become an artist or a dancer. Volunteer with younger kids.

When you feel like you're getting a little lost in the family crowd, it can help to have something that's all yours.

The baby

The baby of the family (also known as the youngest child) is often the most frustrating sibling for the older kids. They feel as if the baby gets more attention—and gets away with more than they ever could. Sadly, that's usually true. If you're the baby of the family, you've probably learned how to get your older brothers or sisters in trouble, knowing your parents will usually blame them for arguments or problems. You've learned how to talk or charm your way out of punishment. So you can see how that might get a little irritating for the other kids.

As the baby, you really do have it easier sometimes. By the time you came along, your parents had a better idea of what they were doing. Plus, they're more tired and more distracted than they were with your brothers and sisters, so they might not notice every little mistake you make like they did with the older kids. Try not to take advantage of your position in the family. Instead do your best to build good relationships with your siblings. When you get older, you'll appreciate their friendship and wisdom more than you can imagine.

The only child

Most only children have a lot of the characteristics of the oldest child—they try to be perfect and have a strong need to please others. And if you're more than seven years older or younger than your closest sibling, you're probably more like an only child than you might expect. When my (Sissy's) little sister was born, I had been an only child for 16 years. So even though I'm not really an only child anymore, I spent most of my childhood as one.

Only children have one tendency oldest children don't usually have—they can have a hard time working with others. Brothers and sisters help us learn to share and work together. They even teach us how to fight and forgive as a natural part of growing up. Only children don't have that experience. My (Sissy's) mom talks about how I used to invite friends over, have fun with them for a while, and then ask my mom when they were going home. I was ready to have my own space again. Now I wish I had learned how to share and work with other people earlier. I wish I'd been involved in more team sports or other activities that would have taught me how to cooperate a bit better.

If you're an only child, make sure you're in places and groups where you have to learn to work with others. You'll be glad you did—and so will the people you'll work and live with someday.

Think About It

Which role do you play in your family? How does your birth order impact your relationships with your brothers and sisters?

If you asked your siblings what they thought about you, what do you think they'd say?

How can you build stronger relationships with your brothers and sisters?

Sibling rivalry

When things are hard at school—girls are mean, boys are weird—you want to come home and feel safe. Fighting with your brothers and sisters can throw this off. That's one of the big reasons sibling rivalry can be so hard to deal with. If you feel like you and your siblings fight all the time, or if you just want to be closer to them, try these secrets for creating better relationships:

1) Do your part. Don't pick fights when you're upset about something else.
2) Respect each other. Respect each other. Respect each other.
3) Apologize when you hurt your brother or sister—even if it's an accident.
4) If your brother or sister hurts you, talk to him or her about it—calmly.
5) Have fun together.

Your brothers and sisters are very important parts of your day-to-day life. Some of the best memories you'll have of growing up will come from the fun and silliness that can only happen with siblings. It's likely you'll know your brothers and sisters longer than you know anyone else in your life, so it's worth the effort to build strong, healthy relationships with them. So be kind and be forgiving. And remember they're not perfect, either.

Grandparents

We both remember being forced to visit our grandparents when we were growing up. At the time it seemed boring and unnecessary. Now that we're adults, we're both so glad we did that. Your grandparents are valuable parts of your family. And they're part of you, too. They love you in a totally different way from the way your parents love you. Spend time with them. Learn from them. Listen to the stories they tell and enjoy the memories you make together. They won't be around forever, and when they're gone, you'll be so glad you took the time to get to know them.

Extended Family

As you grow up, other adults will come into your life. These might be aunts, uncles, friends of your parents, teachers, godparents, or coaches. Pay attention to these people and find a few who you can look up to. They can become trusted friends who can help you learn more about who you are and who you want to be.

Spend time with these adults. Ask questions. Learn from them. There's an old African saying, "It takes a village to raise a child." These people are your village. They can give you advice when you're having trouble with your parents. They can share a perspective on life that might be very different from your family's perspective. They'll introduce you to new ideas, new activities, new adventures. So make the most of this village of people who care about you.

All of these people we've mentioned in this chapter help shape the person you're becoming. Your life might not include all of them, and that's okay—every family has little holes and squiggles in their family circle. Families are part of the fallen world, too. If your dad isn't in the picture, know God can put other men in your life to stand in his place. If your mom died when you were younger, other women will love you and offer so much of what your mom would have.

You might also have a parent or sibling or grandparent who doesn't act like the people we've been talking about. Maybe your parents are divorced and really angry at each other, and you get caught in the middle. Maybe your mom comes in and out of your life, or your dad drinks too much. You might have a brother who had to be sent away because of all the trouble he's gotten into. You might have grandparents who criticize everything you do.

Most of us have at least one of these squiggles in our family circle. These squiggles don't have anything to do with you. They're not your fault. And it's not your responsibility to fix them. If something feels wrong in your family, talk to a trusted family member or other adult in your life. You may even need to come in and talk to someone like us—a counselor who can help you work through the hurt that comes from these kinds of family situations. Whatever you decide to do about your situation, remember you're not alone—every family has problems. And you have people who care about you and want to help.

God will use all types of people at different times in your life. Be open to what these people have to offer. Watch. Learn. Be patient. Forgive. Respect. Enjoy. Those are some of the secrets we've found to strong family relationships. But the most important secret we can share with you about your family is this: You are loved more than you could ever know.

9

Mile Marker Nine:
FRIENDSHIP SECRETS

God will use all types of people at different times in your life. Be open to what these people have to offer. Watch. Learn. Be patient. Forgive. Respect. Enjoy. Those are the secrets to strong relationships. But the most important secret we can share with you is this: You're loved more than you could ever know.

Feel like you're having a little case of déjà vu? You're right. You just read a paragraph almost exactly like that one. But we didn't repeat it to trick you or see if you're paying attention. We repeated it because those words are just as important in your friendships as they are in your family.

Your friendships will be hard in these next few years. You'll have a lot of uphills and a lot of downhills. It will be a relationship roller coaster—with girls and guys.

In this chapter we want to talk about girls. We'll tackle the guys in the next chapter (well, we won't really tackle them, although some of you might like to when they're driving you crazy!).

You'll experience plenty of ups and downs in your friendships with girls during these years. You will have closer friends than you've ever had before, and you will probably struggle with those friends and other girls more than you ever have before. So here are some thoughts to help you navigate the often-turbulent waters of friendship.

We want to help you get ready for the friendship journey you're taking in these years. But rather than only hearing our thoughts, we thought you might like to hear from other girls, too. So we asked girls your age what they wish they knew about friendships with girls and guys. These are their questions—and our secrets. Shhhhhhh!

Why Do Girls Gossip about Each Other?

Wouldn't it be nice if we didn't have to ask this question? But we do because we do—gossip, that is. The reason we gossip is—in a weird, twisted kind of way—because it makes us feel better. It makes us feel better about ourselves to say something bad about someone else. It also makes us feel connected to someone to have a common enemy (there's that whole need for relationship thing again). For example, you may be sitting beside two girls who are talking about someone you know and don't like much, either. So you jump in and add your negative thoughts about the poor girl. While it tears the other girl to shreds, it makes you feel more connected to the two who were initially doing the tearing. Gossip brings girls together—in a really yucky way.

We all fall into the gossip habit at times. Women gossip, too—a lot of girls never grow out of it. But nothing's good about gossip. The only parts of us that feel better when we do it are the really selfish, insecure parts. There's a great verse in the Bible that gives us some direction on the gossip question. It says, "Do not let any unwholesome talk come out of your mouths, but only what is helpful for building others up according to their needs, that it may benefit those who listen" (Ephesians 4:29).

Be different. Stand up for your friends. Stand out because you're someone who is more concerned about what other people need and feel than about making yourself look good. You will end up looking—and feeling—much better if you do.

If one of your friends talks behind your back, the best thing to do is go to that friend and get the truth. Without accusing her, tell her what you heard. Let her explain her side of the story. It could be you've had a huge misunderstanding. If she denies gossiping about you but you're certain she did, go ahead and tell her you know. And tell her you forgive her. Forgiveness helps her, and it helps you not to hold on to the anger.

If you have a friend who talks behind your back, she might not be the kind of friend you want to spend a lot of time with—or at least trust with things that are important to you. If she's talked behind your back and you've talked to her several times, it might be better just to give her space. But don't talk about her to your friends— that's repaying evil for evil, something the Bible warns us about: "Do not repay evil with evil or insult with insult. On the contrary, repay evil with blessing, because to this you were called so that you may inherit a blessing" (1 Peter 3:9).

Why Do Girls Act Differently toward You When They're around Guys?

Girls sometimes act differently toward you when they're around guys because they're thinking more about the guys than about you. Some of this is normal. Any girl can get distracted when a boy she likes looks her way. But you don't want to make a habit of it. A lot of girls lose friends in middle school and high school because they drop their friends whenever guys come along. You don't want to be one of those girls.

Why? Because with the exception of the guy you marry someday, your girlfriends will be part of your life a lot longer than some guy. Your girlfriends are special, so treat them that way. If you have a friend who does the dropping, you can kindly pull her aside and tell her how you feel. If she's a good friend, she'll want to know she hurt you. She might be a little defensive at first, but a true friend will eventually want to work it out.

How Should I Deal with Cliques in School?

Don't you wish they just weren't there? But they are—and they will be for a little while longer. It does get better when you get to high school, although you can still find cliques there, too. For now, though, they're just part of being in middle school.

The best way to deal with cliques is the best way to deal with people in general—be kind. There's a difference, though, between kindness and servitude. You shouldn't have to earn your way into friendship. So if you want to be part of some group, don't be so desperate to get in that you offer to do their homework or buy their lunch. They'll see right through your efforts to fit in. And really, do you want friends who only like you when you do something for them? Real friends like you because you're you, not because you do them favors.

One of the big problems with cliques is they make you feel like maybe the friends you have aren't good enough. But unless your current friends are unkind or a bad influence, you could hurt a lot of feelings by giving up one group of friends for another.

If you don't have many friends, don't set your sights on belonging to the popular group. Find the girls who have reputations of being the nice ones in school. They're easier to be friends with and will usually treat you with kindness. You can also find friends through after-school activities, a youth group at your church, or just about any other place where you're doing something you enjoy. Having a common interest is a great foundation for building a new friendship.

If girls are mean to you, talk to your mom, a school counselor, or another adult you trust. They can usually give you good insight on how to deal with the problem. Most adults—including us—know the best way to deal with mean girls is to be kind and avoid them when you can. Don't try to win them over—if they're mean, they're likely to turn on you even after you've made friends with them. But you can still be kind because you want to be a kind person, regardless of how other people treat you.

> *It's important to be who God made you to be and not just do what other people do—because you're not being yourself, and it's just uncomfortable.—Hope, 15*

If you find you're actually *in* the mean group, you have a tough choice to make. You can stick with those friends and try to influence them to be nicer, or you can find a new group of friends. And honestly, you're probably better off moving on to new friends. Just by hanging around with mean girls, you will get a reputation as a mean girl yourself.

Something interesting happens in the popularity picture as you get older. Right now the people who are the most popular are often popular because they're cute or wild or so mean other people are too afraid of them not to pay attention to them. But as you get older, the nice girls become more popular. Hang in there and wait for that. I (Sissy) remember sitting on top of the jungle gym talking to my friend in sixth grade about how badly we wanted to be popular. But I'm glad I wasn't. At my school the popular girls were mean and quickly got the worst reputations. Things got much better in high school. I was a part of a very sweet group of girls who other people liked, not because they were afraid of us but because they respected us.

Why Are Girls Jealous of Other Girls' Successes?

Girls have a hard time being glad for each other when good things happen, mostly because we want those good things for ourselves. We all feel this way at some point or another. If you feel it a lot, though, you might want to pray about it. Talk to your mom or someone older about it, too. God can change your heart to make you more generous than jealous.

Your friends will feel jealous of you from time to time, too. This is normal. They might even tell you every once in a while. But if you have a friend who gets jealous every time something good comes your way or gets really angry about it, you may need to distance yourself from that friend. You want friends who, even though they may have a hard time, will still try to be encouraging and happy for you when things go well. Those friends are out there—they may just be a little harder to find.

How Do I Know If My Friends Really Like Me for Who I Am?

One of the best ways to tell if your friends like you for who you are is to be yourself—then see if they're still around. One of the worst ways to tell is when you ask them, "What's wrong?" or, "Are you mad at me?" every time they're quiet or act a little different than usual. Usually, the reason your friends are quiet has to do with them, not you. And it just bothers them more if you keep asking.

Trust is one of the hardest things to learn at any age. But if your friends are still your friends—if they talk to you, call you, sit by you, or ask you to do something every once in a while—they probably like you for who you are.

If your friends like to tell you how you should change or how they think you should be acting different, they're not really your friends—at least not the kind of friends you want. You might be familiar with Galinda from the Broadway musical *Wicked*. She loved to make all kinds of improvements to help her friends become popular. Galinda was not the kind of friend Elphaba (also known as the Wicked Witch of the West) needed—and not the kind of friend you need, either (although she was hysterical and eventually learned to love Elphaba just the way she was). You want and need friends who will like you for you and encourage you to be more of the person God made you.

What Are Good Qualities to Look for in a Friend?

The best kinds of friends are those who are loyal, who will stand up for you no matter the cost, who are kind to you. Good friends encourage you and tell you when you do something well. They gently challenge you when you do something that's not true to who you are or what you believe. They like you for who you are. They're people you can laugh with—without laughing at someone else. They bring out the best in you. They make you want to be a better person just by the way they treat you.

These are great qualities in a friend. But remember, there's no such thing as a perfect friend, except for God. Even the best of friends will hurt or disappoint you sometimes. But you can still look for those friends who you can enjoy and care about and who will grow with you toward God and toward being the people he made you both to be.

What's the Best Way to Make and Keep Friends?

The best way to make a friend is to be a friend. Think about what you want in a friend, then act that way. Don't do things to other people that would be hurtful to you. Take initiative. We know a lot of girls who feel no one likes them, but the reality is, they haven't done much to try to make friends. You can't wait for someone to come to you and ask for your friendship. They might be shy, too. If you want to be friends with someone, sit by her at lunch. Talk to her. Ask her questions. Get to know her over the course of a few weeks. If it seems like you have some things in common, great! If not, don't try too hard to make it work or follow her around to try to make her your best friend.

Girls like other girls who are confident in who they are and don't look desperate to have friends. We all feel desperate sometimes, but that's something you tell someone when you know them really well. Until then, it's our friendship secret.

What's the Best Way to Tell a Friend When She's Hurt Your Feelings?

The best way to tell your friends anything is always to assume the best about them. What this means is this: If Ginny said something that really hurt your feelings, you could assume Ginny is mad at you. Or you could assume Ginny was just having a bad day and didn't mean to hurt you at all.

Remember those hiccups in confidence we talked about? They make it easy to assume the worst about Ginny—she meant to hurt your feelings, she doesn't like you anymore, no one really does. (This is completely untrue, but we think this way sometimes, don't we?) If you believed this, it would be easy to get mad at Ginny. Then she would probably feel attacked and get mad back.

But a better way to deal with this kind of situation is: Go up to Ginny and say, "Hey, Ginny, I know you said _____ earlier. That didn't really sound like something you would normally say. I was just wondering if you were okay. It hurt my feelings, but I don't think you meant to. I'm worried about you." That assumes the best about Ginny.

Trust your friends. Talk to them with kindness and humility even—maybe especially—when they hurt you. It will be much easier to work things out and much harder to be angry at each other.

Why Does It Seem Like You're Best Friends One Week and Enemies the Next?

A good word for this is *fickle*. Fickle is when you constantly change your mind about what you like, who you like, and who your firends are. It's fine to be fickle with a favorite shirt or a favorite TV show. But being fickle about friends creates a lot of heartache for everyone. It hurts when someone is fickle about you, and it hurts when you're fickle about someone else. But it happens, especially in middle school. We can assure you this gets better in high school, too.

Middle school girls don't really mean to be fickle. At this age, girls are trying to figure out who they are and who they want to be friends with. So they'll switch groups and even personalities in the process. Maybe you've done some of that yourself. If you find yourself hanging around with friends who just don't seem to be the right fit for you, there's nothing wrong with making some new friends. But you don't have to dump your old friends completely. You can still be kind, get together now and then, and let them know you still like them.

If you're on the receiving end of someone else's fickleness, hang in there. Every girl wants to find friends who will stick by her, but sometimes that can take awhile. If your friend comes and goes once a week, she might not be the best kind of friend. But be patient. You'll find friends who will stick by you. They're a little hard to find right now, but you can pray and tell God what you want and how you feel. He cares even when it seems as if no one else does.

Friendships will create many of the uphills you face during this stage of your life. Knowing they get easier can help you get through these years. So don't give up on finding good friends. Ask God to bring kind, honest, faithful friends into your life. And ask God to help you be that kind of friend to the girls around you. No matter who you're friends with, you can still be the kind, generous girl God made you.

Think About It

What other struggles do you have with your girl friends? Who can you talk to about those struggles?

Do you struggle with jealousy or fickleness when it comes to your friends? Why do you think you feel that way? How can you start feeling more secure and confident with your friends? How can you learn to be a better friend? How can you reach out to someone who needs a friend?

10

Mile Marker Ten:
THE SECRET LIFE OF BOYS

This chapter is all about boys. They sometimes feel like the biggest secret to us, mostly because we don't understand them. Why did your best friend, the guy you rode bikes with every day, start acting weird around you? Why does the boy who sits behind you in math class pick on you? How should you act around a boy you think is cute? Girls have all these questions and more when it comes to understanding these confusing guys.

Boys are confusing because they're so different from us. They think and talk and joke around and communicate differently than we do. While they go through some of the same changes girls experience during these years—puberty, changing relationships, new ideas about who they are and what they want out of life—the changes affect them in a whole different way. This chapter is meant to explain why the guys you know are changing and why your feelings about them might be changing, too. Our hope is telling you these secrets about boys can help you build strong, healthy relationships with the guys in your life.

First we want to give you some instructions on how to read this chapter. As we've said before, we all develop—physically and emotionally—at different speeds. This means some girls start to think about boys in an "I-really-like-him-as-more-than-a-friend" kind of way in sixth grade. Some girls at this stage don't get what the big deal is and have no interest in the boy craziness they see in other girls. There's no right way to think when it comes to boys.

Because of that, we've divided this chapter into three sections based on how you feel about boys:

1) Not really interested in more than riding bikes and playing tag.
2) I'm starting to be interested in boys, but I'm a little confused.
3) I'm going out with someone—or would like to be.

Each section has a list of questions from real girls your age. But we're not going to answer the questions. Instead we decided to let boys speak for themselves since they're the only ones who really understand their secrets. We chose guys we think are great. They're really smart and cute—the kind of guys you'd want for big brothers. Most of them are in high school and college, which means they've learned a lot about friendship and girls since they were in middle school. And that makes their answers even better—they've made it through the bumpy years and learned a lot in the process.

So are you ready to find out more about the secret life of boys? Okay, here we go!

Not So Interested

Why do boys act like they're my friends one minute and then ignore me the next, especially in front of their friends?

Guys want to look cool. So we try really hard to impress our guy friends. And guys make fun of each other—especially when it comes to girls. That's why we make fun of you or just ignore you when we're around other guys, but are nice to you when we're by ourselves. The way we act when we're by ourselves is usually a better sign of how we really feel about you.

If you have a guy friend who does this, try talking to him about it. Or you can just give him a little more space when he's around his friends and trust that even if he's acting like a goofball, he still wants to be your friend—he's just a goofball who doesn't have the maturity to show you how he feels. We do grow out of this—or at least become a little more aware of it as we get older.

Why do my good guy friends treat me differently than they used to?

You may have noticed guys stop being as competitive with you or stop letting you play with them when they're doing "guy" things. It's because girls are as confusing to us as we are to you. And all of a sudden our parents are telling us we need to act like gentlemen and we're supposed to treat girls a certain way. We used to treat you like one of us, so we don't really know how to treat you now. Instead we just get awkward, which you probably need to get used to because we do that a lot.

What should I do if a boy likes me, and I just like him as a friend?

Tell him nicely. Boys like it when girls tell them the truth rather than just act awkward (we know, we know—it's not fair we get to be awkward but don't want you to be) or avoid us. We'll respect you if you're honest. But don't tell us you want to be friends and then not be our friend. That hurts our feelings, and a lot of girls do that just to get out of the situation. Tell us the truth and be kind. That's really always the best answer with us.

Why do guys tease girls?

We're used to teasing other guys. It's our way of talking to other guys, and it spills over into how we talk to you. Plus, we're trying to impress you. The problem is we don't really know how to talk to you—or at least talk like girls talk to each other. So we usually start with teasing to try to get your attention. You can help us talk about other things—ask us questions, try to get to know us. We'll usually catch on.

Why do boys pick on and annoy their sisters?

Most of the time it's because we can. We usually grow out of this, but for now it's fun to get a reaction—it makes us laugh when you scream or try to hit us. It's more like a game to us. The best way to get us to stop is to ignore us.

Interested but Confused
What do guys look for in a girl?

The most important thing we look for is you being yourself. We don't want you to try to impress us (even though we might do all kinds of goofy stuff to impress you). Because we're all different, we like different types of girls. Some guys like sportier girls, some guys like smarter girls, and so on. But the kind of girls all guys (or at least the good ones) really like are girls we respect and who are themselves. Don't try to look less smart or less athletic or less anything than you are. We don't like that. We like you to be you.

Why do guys sometimes get awkward or show off in front of the girls they like?

We definitely do both of these. We get awkward and show off because we like you—and we don't really know what to do. We're trying to impress you and make you like us. We think if we look cool or funny, you might like us better. And then we just get awkward because we really don't know how to be cool or funny. Really, we're just insecure and are either trying to show off to make you think we're not insecure, or hiding behind jokes and goofiness because we're scared you'll see how insecure we are.

How do guys try to impress girls?

It's a little different for every guy, but showing off is definitely something most of us do. We might try to be good at sports or try to be funny. We might tease you—which we know is kind of stupid (we tease each other, too). We also try to act like we don't really care what you think about us—even though we care a lot. And every once in a while we do something nice, like write you a note or give you a present.

How can you talk to your crush?

(It's me, Melissa. I'm breaking in on the boys to tell you a story. When I was 11, I had a crush on a senior in high school. One night at a basketball game I wedged my way in to sit beside him in the bleachers. Then I took out my camera and took his picture. I was sitting right next to him, and I think the flash nearly blinded him. This kind of crush is best enjoyed from afar. Now back to the guys.)

If your crush is closer to your age, just talk to him. Don't talk too much and please don't walk up to us and giggle—that drives us crazy. Just say "hi" and ask us something like, "How was your weekend?" or, "What did you think about that test?" Just be normal, be yourself. If you want us to like you for you, then you have to act like you, not some giggly, silly version of yourself.

Going Out or Would Like to Be
Why do guys get other guys to ask girls out?

Once again we're scared. Guys are terrified of being rejected. So if someone else asks you out for us, the rejection doesn't hurt quite so much—or at least you don't have to see us being rejected. But we will—or should—grow out of it. Guys in high school will ask you out themselves. If they don't, you probably don't want to go out with them anyway.

If a girl likes a guy, should she tell him?
What should she do?

Guys like to take the initiative. God made us that way. We feel better about ourselves when we're the ones pursuing you, even though it scares us to death. So we might like it if you tell us you like us, but if you keep doing it, it gets really old. We like you more if you maybe give us clues but don't tell us straight out. You can talk to us; hang out with us at school (but please don't follow us around—that's coming on too strong). Just be nice to us. That way we know it's safe to pursue you, but we still get to do the pursuing.

(Sissy here: One guy your age said, "Girls should never, ever ask a guy out." How's that for being honest?)

How do you deal with girls who flirt a lot?

We might like it in the beginning, but it gets old fast. Those girls usually aren't the ones we want to have real relationships with. We want to have a little bit of a challenge. Guys like girls who are kind of mysterious. If you flirt all the time, it's too easy for us—it takes all the mystery away.

How does what a girl wears affect how you think about her?

It tells us a lot about the girl. If a girl wears really tight or revealing clothes, it makes us think more about what she looks like than who she is. Guys really struggle with this, but we don't want to. We want to like you for who you are, not what you look like. When we see girls who are Christians and who dress like that, we're actually really disappointed—we thought they were trying to help us stay pure. You can still dress pretty and dress in a way that doesn't make us only think about your looks.

What's a good first date? Would you kiss a girl on a first date, or would you get to know her better?

First of all, you don't need to be dating yet. You have a lot of time to do that—and usually, the girls who date a lot are not the ones guys really want to have relationships with. But when you do start dating, you want the guy to come to your house and pick you up. You want to be with a guy who really respects you. He'll show respect by coming to the door to pick you up, meeting your parents, opening the door for you, and offering to pay for your date. Go somewhere you can talk and get to know each other, like out for pizza or to a coffee shop. Movies are fun, but they don't give you much chance to get to know each other.

As far as the kiss goes, make him wait. Don't let him kiss you on the first date—and definitely don't let him kiss you before that. If you want to be the kind of girl a guy wants to date, you have to act like the kind of girl a guy wants to have a real relationship with. If you want guys to respect you, you have to act in a way that helps you earn respect. In the long run a guy will like you—and you'll like yourself—a whole lot more.

Think About It

How have your feelings about boys changed in the last year? Write down some of the questions you have about the guys in your life. How do these questions impact your friendships with guys?

Worth the Wait

Do you remember when we said relationships are often the very best and worst things to happen to us? As girls we want to be close and connected—to girls and guys. Pray for God to bring girls and guys into your life who bring out the best in you. You need people your age who will walk beside you and encourage and challenge you to be more of who God made you to be. Be yourself. Be the kind of person you would want to have as a friend. The kind of friends—girls and guys—you want to have in your life are out there. And they're definitely worth the wait!

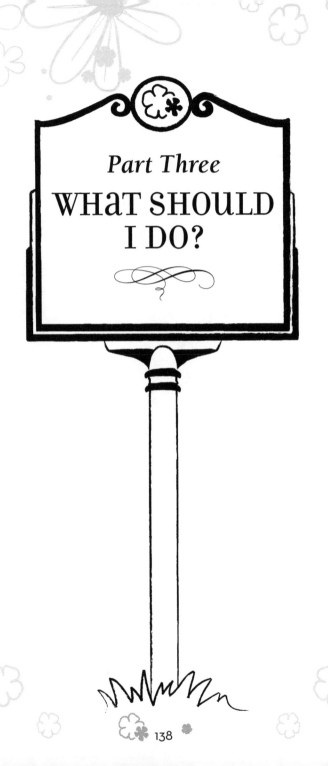

Part Three

WHAT SHOULD I DO?

11

Mile Marker Eleven:
pressure

Pressure. Every girl feels it. You might feel pressure about school, sports, keeping up with your friends, or staying thin. You might even be starting to feel some pressure about alcohol or drugs. A lot of confusing situations will be coming at you in these next few years, and we want to help you navigate your way through them. This chapter is about the biggies—the pressures that seem hardest for girls your age.

In each section of the chapter we'll talk about a particular source of pressure—we're going to call it "What they say." "They" are the things and people that influence what you believe about who you are and who you should be. This includes the messages you hear and see in magazines, on TV, through movies and music, and from your friends. Then we'll talk about specific ways you can deal with the pressure "they" put on you. These sections will be called "What you can do." We hope these sections will show you how to be the unique, wonderful, delightful girl God made you to be, no matter what "they" say.

Media
What they say
The media is not only trying to define beauty, but it is also trying to define you. And what media communicates is all about the

way you look and act, rather than who you are. Media messages are so much a part of our lives, after a while we hardly notice them. But that doesn't mean they've stopped affecting the way we think and feel about ourselves.

Think About It

Take some time to consider the teenage girls you see on TV or in movies or magazines. What messages do they give you about how girls your age should look or how you should act? Do those messages match the person you want to be?

Now look over that list of messages and imagine what life would be like if every girl fit that image. Pretty boring, huh? If every teenage girl looked and acted like the media's ideal girl, everyone would have pre-period bodies and the same hairstyles (and colors), and we'd all wear the same clothes and even talk the same way. You'd see no variety, no uniqueness, and no personality in the halls of your school. Everyone would be sarcastic and talk back to their parents and teachers. All the girls would be boy crazy, and all the boys would be—well, just kind of crazy.

Media, Continued
What you can do

Don't give in! Notice and hang on to everything that makes you unique. Find your own sense of style based on what looks good, what's appropriate, and what you can afford. Wear your hair different ways. Explore activities that interest you. Make friends with people who are unique in good ways. Tell your friends what you like about them, focusing on the inside not the outside. Be creative. Volunteer.

Real beauty comes from who you are and how you feel about yourself, not what you look like. Make choices that draw out that kind of beauty.

Watch what you're watching and listening to. Pay attention to the voices you hear and images you see in the media. Notice the kind of choices girls make in the movies and shows you watch and the music you listen to. Do they reflect the kind of girl you want to be? If they don't, you might need to consider getting those images out of your life.

The morals teenage girls typically have in movies, on TV, and in some books are no morals at all. We know it doesn't seem as if these things are affecting you, but over time they will. You'll start to think it's normal to have a steady boyfriend when you're 13 or to dress like an adult woman when you're 12.

This is the time in your life when you're making all kinds of decisions about who you are and who you want to be. So get your advice from real people you trust—your parents, your teachers, your older siblings. Read your Bible. Join a youth group at your church or a Christian club at school. Read magazines like *TeenVirtue* or *Brio* to help you figure out what good choices look like. Work to build a life filled with messages to help you feel good about yourself and honor the person God made you at the same time.

Get to know other girls who don't fit the media's picture of perfection. Make friends with real girls who live in the real world. And take a look at some of the wonderful fictional characters in books and movies and on TV—like Scout in *To Kill a Mockingbird*, Akeelah from *Akeelah and the Bee*, or Raven from *That's So Raven*. These girls break the typical media mold of perfection. Here's a list of other books, music, and movies we think you'll like. They feature girls whose beauty has much more to do with who they are than how they look.

Books
- *A Little Princess* by Frances Hodgson Burnett
- *Anne of Green Gables* series by L.M. Montgomery
- *A Wrinkle in Time* series by Madeleine L'Engle
- *Each Little Bird That Sings* by Deborah Wiles
- *Ida B* by Katherine Hannigan
- *The Chronicles of Narnia* series by C.S. Lewis
- *Little House on the Prairie* series by Laura Ingalls Wilder
- *Nancy Drew* series by Carolyn Keene
- *The Secret Garden* by Frances Hodgson Burnett
- *Tiger Rising* by Kate Dicamillo

Musicians
Bethany Dillon
Amy Grant
Lindsey Kane
Cindy Morgan
Mandisa
Mary Mary
Kelly Minter
ZOEgirl

Movies
- *Akeelah and the Bee*
- *Enchanted*
- *Because of Winn-Dixie*
- *The Sound of Music*
- *The Wizard of Oz*
- *13 Going on 30—especially if you're close to 13*
- *To Kill a Mockingbird*
- *The Sisterhood of the Traveling Pants*
- *Nim's Island*
- *The Chronicles of Narnia*

Communication
What they say

Here's a message we've bet you've picked up on: Every girl has to have a cell phone by the time she's in middle school. And an iPod. And a laptop. And be on MySpace or Facebook or whatever the next big thing is. That's what they—movies and advertisers and all the folks who make and design all those things—tell you. They tell you this because they want you (or your parents) to buy them. And nothing makes you want something more than the idea that everyone else has it. That's why marketing people— the people in charge of selling a product—work really hard to convince you if you don't have their product, you'll be left out.

Of course the marketing people aren't the only ones pressuring you. Your friends probably want you to have all the latest communication tools so they can stay in touch with you all the time. They want to be able to text—or call, IM, or Facebook—you to ask your advice or tell you the latest gossip. "Everyone" has these things for a couple reasons—they're cool, and they help you stay in constant contact with your favorite people. Who wouldn't want that?

What you can do

This is a hard one to deal with because what "they" are saying might not bother you. In fact, you probably wouldn't mind having a cell phone and a laptop and an iPod. You wouldn't mind being allowed on MySpace and Facebook. But your parents are a little more hesitant—and so are we. This is why:

Technology changes you.

Instant access—the kind you get through texting or IMing—changes the way you talk. When you text message, you don't usually take the time to be polite. You don't ask, "How are you?" or say any of the other nice things you would say if you were talking in person. But those nice things are an important part of relating to other people. They're part of being kind and patient.

Technology can give you the wrong kind of freedom.

The way you communicate on the Internet can be very different from the way you communicate face-to-face. We've met with a lot of girls who've gotten in trouble with boys—and their parents—because of the way they talked on the Internet. When you "talk" online, your words can take on meanings you didn't intend. Boys in particular can quickly get the wrong idea. What you think of as being friendly and maybe a little flirty, they might think of as a serious offer. (If you're doing this, then you know exactly what we're talking about.) This kind of conversation can put you in the category of girls boys like to talk to but don't really respect. Be *very* careful how you communicate to boys on the Internet.

We have also talked to a lot of girls who've been unkind to other girls on the Internet—and these are girls who are normally kind. The Internet can make you bold in a way that hurts other people. It's easy to say things online you would never say in person—it's easy to forget you're talking to another human being. But even though you can't hear the hurt in her voice or see it in her eyes, you can make another person feel terrible by what you say to or about her online. Be who you are—and be kind—whether you're talking in person, on the Internet, or on the phone.

There really are scary people on the Internet.

We know a 14-year-old girl who talked to a guy online for a long time. He told her he was 17 and he thought she was amazing. She thought they were in love and arranged to meet him in person. Somehow her dad found out about it and tracked the guy down. It turns out he was the same age as her dad and had a daughter a year older than her. Yuck! And we can promise you; he didn't have anything good in mind when he agreed to meet our friend. She could have ended up in a lot of trouble—or even danger. There are a lot of weird people like this man out there. So don't talk to people online unless you know them in person. Period.

Being first isn't always best.

This may sound strange, but we've discovered that the girl who's the first one to have a cell phone, the first one to be on MySpace or Facebook, the first one to date, often ends up with a bad reputation—even if she doesn't deserve it. You don't want this kind of reputation. It's good to have things to look forward to as you get older. Trust us—-and your parents. Remember, they're smarter than you think.

School Culture: Athletics and Academics
What they say
When our friend Anne was 12, her parents noticed she was washing her hands a lot. This kind of "a lot" wasn't just before meals

or after using the restroom. This was washing her hands 15-to-20-times-a-day "a lot." Something was going on with Anne.

When her parents asked her about it, Anne didn't really know why she was doing this. But what Anne did know was, she felt stressed. Anne was one of the forwards on her school soccer team and was about to go to the state tournament. She earned really good grades but was disappointed with a couple of Bs she'd gotten on her last report card. She also wanted to try out for the school play but couldn't figure out how to fit that in with her busy schedule. Anne was worried she was disappointing her parents, her coach, even her friends who wanted her to be in the play with them. She was stressed and feeling pressure from every angle.

Maybe you understand how Anne felt. Not only do you want to feel good about your grades and your performance in sports, but you also want other people to feel good about them. It's as if we have a built-in need to please other people.

Actually, we do. It's part of being created for relationships. We want to do well. We want to please our parents and our friends. We want to please God. And because we want to please everyone, we expect a lot from ourselves—sometimes too much. Rather than expecting our best, we expect perfection. And that's way too much pressure.

Anne responded to the pressure by washing her hands a lot. It felt like a way to have some control over what was happening in her life. Other girls react to intense pressure by eating too much—or not enough. Some girls stop sleeping well—or sleep too much. Some girls start to shut out their friends and family; other girls throw themselves into everything. Some girls cry more often; other girls yell more often. Each girl reacts to this pressure to be perfect in a different way.

Think About It

How do you react to pressure?

How much of the pressure you feel comes from other people?

How much of it comes from yourself and your expectations?

How can you adjust your expectations of yourself so you can feel a little less stress? What are some ways you can let go of the pressure? What helps you relax?

What you can do

Remind yourself perfection isn't possible—for anyone. You can be a great athlete and set all kinds of records, but even the best athletes fail sometimes. You can earn straight As, but still get an 89 once in a while. No one can excel all the time.

God doesn't want your perfection—God wants your heart. God wants you to do the best you can, but God also knows you will fail sometimes. And you know what? Those are the moments when God can help you grow the most. If you were always perfect, you wouldn't have much left to learn. And that would get really boring. God has so much to show you, so much to teach you, and the best learning will often come through failure.

Know the difference between being kind and living to please people. You can be kind and make choices that fit in with who you believe God made you to be—that's your responsibility. Making other people happy isn't. Sometimes you'll have to choose between two good things—like a track meet and a school play. Either your coach or your drama teacher will be disappointed. But they are grown-ups and will learn to work it out.

This doesn't mean you should do whatever you want no matter what other people think. But when you're doing your best, that's all you can do. Sometimes your parents or teachers or coaches will believe your best is more than you're doing—and you probably know when they're right. You know when you haven't worked very hard on a project or have been taking it easy during practice or haven't paid attention in class. Doing your best means giving a project or practice or class your best effort. If you're still not sure what your best looks like, think about these words from the apostle Paul: "Whatever you do, work at it with all your heart, as working for the Lord, not for human masters" (Colossians 3:23). Put your heart into whatever you do, and you'll most likely be giving it your best effort.

Your best effort, however, is different from perfection. Don't expect perfection from yourself and don't live to please other people. Instead live to honor God—with honesty, hard work, and an openness to learning the lessons that can sometimes come through failure.

Drugs and Alcohol

What they say

The messages about drugs and alcohol are going to be different for every girl and at every age. You may get to be 14—or older—before you ever see someone your age use drugs or alcohol. We both did. But I (Sissy) sure heard about it. Those girls—who happened to be the first in my class to get to do things—were also the first in the class to start drinking. But even if you're not around these things yet, this section will help you gain confidence for the time when you are.

If you are around drugs and alcohol, you know what those messages say. They say it's fun to drink. They say drugs will make you feel better. Or maybe they don't say anything. They just make drinking or doing drugs look like the coolest thing in the world.

What you can do

Stay away from it. You'll never have a good reason to drink before you're legally old enough, and there's never, ever a good reason to take illegal drugs. If you feel like you have to do these things to make other people like you, then those are not people you need as friends. Good friends—and good guys—will never ask you to do something you don't want to do or something dangerous or illegal. And people who are truly worth having as friends—and boyfriends—will like you better for avoiding this stuff. They know it only leads to trouble.

The crowd getting into these things now will get into more things later—more drinking, more dangerous drugs, more high-risk activities. Their parents will find out, the school will find out, their friends' parents will find out. Then these kids will be the ones other parents don't want their kids hanging out with. These kids will get kicked off sports teams and out of extracurricular activities. These kids will have reputations for the rest of their school years, and the reputations won't be good. You don't want to be one of these kids.

Remember—doing drugs or drinking alcohol doesn't make you feel better. People act as if it's fun to drink or take drugs, as if these substances help you let go of all your problems and just enjoy life. But drugs and alcohol only create more problems because they make you lose control. They make you embarrass yourself. They make you say and do things you would never do if you had a clear head. They muddy your thinking so other people can do things to you you'd never allow if you were in control of the situation. Your parents will stop trusting you, and your friends will stop respecting you. And all of that will make you feel terrible.

Find a group of friends who will encourage you to stay away from all of this. Connect with other girls who are making good choices—if you don't know who they are, try joining a Christian club at school or your church. Get involved in a small group where you can help each other stay committed to pursuing a relationship with Jesus. Knowing what your values are and having a group of friends with similar values are the two best ways to avoid drugs and alcohol.

Tell yourself they're not worth it. They're illegal. They're harmful. They're bad ideas. Enough said.

Hurting Yourself

What they say

You may have heard about other girls who hurt themselves physically. You may have even done this yourself because you believe hurting on the outside is better than hurting on the inside. Or maybe that's what "they" have told you.

In this case "they" are probably other kids at school. Maybe you have friends who hurt themselves when they're sad or angry. Maybe you've heard about it on television or in a movie. Maybe you've even read about it in a book. Regardless of who "they" are, if they're telling you hurting yourself physically is a good way to handle any type of problem—they're wrong.

> *I wish I had known the hard times won't last forever—and how important it is to listen to people who love you when they warn you about something.*
> *—Becca, 15*

What you can do

Talk. Hurting yourself might seem like it makes your problems go away, but it only makes life a lot harder. The best way to deal with the issues bothering you is to talk about them. We know that can be hard sometimes. But it truly is the best way to feel better. So talk to your parents. If something makes it hard to talk to them, or if they're the problem you need to talk about, meet with your school counselor, a teacher, or another adult you trust.

If you don't have anyone you feel safe talking to, ask your parents to take you to a counselor. It's important for you to have someone in your life to whom you can say anything. And there's nothing embarrassing about seeing a counselor.

They're pretty cool (if we do say so ourselves!).

Find other ways to let your feelings out. Talking is great, but you can also work through your feelings by writing. So journal. Write poetry or songs. Or use art—paint, draw, sculpt—to get your emotions out. Expressing what you feel is healthy and good for you. Keeping your feelings buried inside is not.

Don't hurt yourself to get attention. Causing yourself pain is a serious problem. It's not something you want to play around with because you feel left out or want people to notice you. I (Sissy) used to act mad at my friends just to get them to pay attention to me. I (Melissa) used to act like a goofball for the same reason. Of course you want attention, but the rest of the world sees hurting yourself as a very real cry for help. If you want attention, get it by being yourself—work hard at school, get involved in activities you enjoy, be a good friend.

If you truly need help and don't know what to do, ask an adult you trust for advice. You are a unique, amazing, wonderful girl, and no one should ever cause you pain, especially yourself.

Body Image
What they say
Unfortunately, you'll find a lot of "theys" out there on this one: Magazines, movies, and television shows; other girls you wish you looked like; other kids who make insensitive comments at school. "They" can even be your parents who mean well but sometimes say things that hurt.

No matter who's sending the message, it tends to be the same one: You don't look like you should. You're too tall, too short, too fat, too skinny, too muscular, not muscular enough. Your thighs are too big, your arms are too thin, your feet are too big, your eyes are too small. The list just keeps going and going.

What you can do

What you look like is only a very small part of who you are. Your beauty has much more to do with your heart than it does with your physical appearance. You probably know other girls who would be much prettier if they were kinder or less selfish or if they smiled once in a while.

Don't compare yourself to other girls. It doesn't help. Ever. You'll end up feeling bad about yourself and disliking other girls because you're jealous of them. So try to remember, just as God gave you a personality unlike anyone else's, God gave you a unique body, too. Trying to make your body something it isn't will leave you unhappy and unhealthy. Having the "perfect" body doesn't make you more valuable or more lovable— not to God, not to anyone.

Exercise. You've probably heard adults say this—your gym teacher, your parents, your coach. Well, once again they're right. (We've said that a lot in this book, haven't we?) Exercise not only helps keep your body healthy, but it also actually releases chemicals in your brain to make you feel good about yourself. You should try to be physically active for at least 30 minutes five days a week. You can take a walk, kick a soccer ball with a friend, dance in your room, or help clean your house (we know you love that option). Being active is the best way to stay healthy.

Don't use food as a way of making bad feelings go away. Food and emotions should be two totally separate things. But sometimes we eat because we feel bad inside. Or we don't eat because we feel bad inside. If you're upset about something, eating a whole bag of chips won't make the problem go away.

And if your life feels out of control, not eating even though you're hungry won't make life more manageable. We've said it before: Let your emotions out by talking, writing, drawing, even praying. Don't ignore your feelings—deal with them.

Be smart about managing your weight. If you want to change your weight, talk to your parents. They can take you to a nutritionist who can help you come up with healthy meal plans. Or they can help you get on a diet and exercise plan that will give you the strength and energy you need to be healthy. A lot of diets deprive your brain of everything it needs to work properly. Your body actually needs a certain amount of food—including fat—to function the way it's supposed to.

If you think about food all the time, don't want to eat, or make yourself throw up, please tell your parents. Ask them to take you to a counselor who can help you figure out why you're feeling this way. You can't deal with this alone. Many people know a lot about girls and food issues. They can help you be healthy and find confidence in yourself at the same time.

If you have a friend who you think might be having some problems with her eating habits, talk to her. She's probably really hurting and doesn't know how to handle. If she won't talk to you, let a counselor at school know about your concerns. The counselor can talk to your friend without letting her know you said anything.

Be Yourself

You will feel all kinds of pressure in these years. A lot of voices will be telling you what you should and shouldn't do. Which ones will you listen to? That's up to you. But the best way to figure out who you want to listen to is to remember who you want to be (which happens to be what we're talking about in the next part of the book). The choices you make now will have a lasting impact on who you are and how other people see you. So don't let all those voices push you into decisions you know aren't right for you. Know what you believe, and and be who you believe you can be. Talk to people when you're struggling. Most of all stay close to God who loves you no matter what.

Part Four

WHO DO I
WANT TO BE?

12

Mile Marker Twelve:
THROWING FRUIT

"You should be ashamed of yourself." Did anybody ever say that to you when you were younger? What do you think they meant? Most likely, you had just done something wrong—took something that wasn't yours, pushed your sister, ate candy when you weren't supposed to, pulled the cat's tail—some little kid-sized crime.

But we would guess most of the time you didn't really feel shame. Maybe you did for the moment, but it went away as soon as your punishment was over. That's not what shame is. If you have felt shame, you don't forget it so easily. We both remember very vividly the first time we felt real, humiliating, can't-believe-I'm-capable-of-such-things shame.

We (Melissa's family) were at my grandmother's house. Everyone was sitting around—aunts, uncles, grandparents, cousins—everybody. I was sitting in a chair just listening to the adults talk. My two-year-old brother, Kim, quietly toddled over to me. He looked up at me, smiled, and with his little hand, took my finger. I watched him as he chomped on my finger as hard as he possibly could. I was shocked. But what I did next startled me even more.

Without thinking I raised my hand and slapped him— hard. Everyone stared at me. I couldn't believe I had just done that—slapped my little brother. And neither could anyone else. I'd never hit him before and certainly never hit him again. But it just happened. I did it. Some kind of anger I'd never even known was inside of me welled up and spewed out at Kim. Kim started crying, my parents got really mad, and all I wanted to do was run.

I (Sissy) remember being 12 and my mom waking me up in the middle of the night—or at least what felt like the middle of the night. It was really probably eight in the morning—which I thought was entirely too early. She woke me up because she had to run some errands and didn't think it was safe for me to be sleeping alone in the house. I thought my mom was kind of a safety nerd. (I didn't know the family secret about a mom's level of intelligence yet.) So she woke me up and walked me to our neighbors, the Longs. She wanted me to stay there while she was gone.

> *I wish I had known to let God help me through life and not to worry so much about everything.*
> —Elaine, 16

I walked across the street in my pajamas and was going to get right back in bed at the Long's house. But my mom started talking. I don't remember what she said—probably something like, "Now you do whatever Mrs. Long tells you to do. Be nice and clean up after yourself"—you know, mom things. But in my exhausted and cranky mind, she went on and on and on. All I wanted to do was go back to sleep.

At some point during what was really probably a three-minute conversation I snapped. I remember getting furious. I started screaming at my mom and ended with, "Would you just get out of here and leave me alone?"

I didn't usually talk to my mom this way. I loved my mom, and even though I got irritated with her from time to time, I really tried to be respectful. But something happened to me that day. I still remember the feeling. It was what counselors and other adults call rage—serious, out-of-control, "I-hate-you" kind of anger. I also remember the feeling that came after. It was shame. I was shocked and embarrassed and couldn't believe I was capable of that kind of fury toward my mom. I wanted to run—just like Melissa.

Have you ever done something that made you want to run or made you feel that kind of shame? Not over a little kid-sized crime, but over something that hurt someone else—something maybe you still even regret to this day? If you have, you're not alone. We all have moments we'd like to go back and change, moments where we've hurt someone we love, said something we regret, or done something we never believed we would ever do in a million years. The Bible says, "All have sinned and fall short of the glory of God" (Romans 3:23). All. That means the girl in your class who looks like she's perfect and has it all together makes huge mistakes. The guy who's cute and cool and acts like nothing ever bothers him does things he knows he shouldn't. Your teachers, your parents, us, you—we all mess up.

We're not talking about the kinds of messes you don't mean to make—like forgetting your backpack on the bus or bumping into your little sister by accident. We mean those moments when you're determined to win at all costs. When you care more about how you feel at the time than about how the other person will feel afterward. When you lose control and your rage comes out all over someone else. We mean the times you hurt someone—and not by accident. Those times when you do something you know you shouldn't, and all you want to do afterward is run.

In those moments—at least soon after those moments—we all would like to say, "That's not me! That's not who I am!" And sometimes it's not. We're hurt or angry or scared so we act in ways we normally wouldn't. But we also all know sometimes that mean, spiteful, selfish person is exactly who we are.

We all sin. But another very important *all* is in the Bible: "For Christ also suffered once for sins, the righteous for the unrighteous, to bring you to God. He was put to death in the body but made alive in the Spirit" (1 Peter 3:18). We all have shame and feel bad about ourselves as a result of sin. But when Christ died on the cross, he died for *all* of us and for *all* of our sins. Our unrighteousness was replaced by his righteousness (that means holiness). Our sin was replaced by his goodness. All of the shame and ugliness and awfulness inside us died with Christ. Once—and for all.

Rotten Fruit

Have you ever stuck your hand into a bowl of fruit and pulled out something rotten? You were expecting a nice red, hard, crunchy apple and got a soft, brown one instead? Maybe it even had bugs flying around it. Once you picked it up, you noticed the smell—the awful, strong stench of something rotten. And you threw it away fast.

The Bible talks a lot about fruit—good fruit and bad fruit. The bad fruit is rotten. It's all the things we don't want anyone to know about. Our selfishness and sin have the same yucky stench as rotten fruit. The great news of the Bible is: Jesus has already thrown out the rotten fruit in our lives. Through his death and resurrection, Jesus defeated sin. And when sin was defeated, our sins—every last one of them—were forgiven.

Jesus also helps us figure out how to have less rotten fruit—less sin—in our lives. It starts with something called *repentance*. Repentance is kind of like turning around. It's as if you're going down the road on your bike, and you suddenly realize you're heading the wrong direction. Naturally, you turn around and go the other way. When it comes to sin, repentance means knowing you've hurt someone—and hurt God, too. It is deciding the angry—or selfish or whatever rotten type of person you were—is not who you want to be, then turning around and doing something different.

Jesus' life showed us how we are supposed to live—with kindness, compassion, generosity, and love. His life was the ultimate mile marker for our journey through life. Jesus showed us the right way to go, so we're able to see when we're heading in the wrong direction. And because Jesus died and was raised from the dead, sin lost its power over us. That means Jesus not only shows us when we're going the wrong way, but he also gives us the strength to turn around.

A Good, Hard Toss

At camp last summer we talked about our rotten fruit. We didn't just kind of halfway mention it in a vague kind of way. We really talked about it. Each person there talked about things she did that were gross and rotten and she was truly ashamed of.

During this talk a bowl was sitting in the front of the room. In this bowl were 35 pieces of rotten fruit—one for each person there. After we talked about our sin, we read a passage from the Bible:

> Where is the god who can compare with you— wiping the slate clean of guilt, turning a blind eye, a deaf ear, to the past sins of your purged and precious people? You don't nurse your anger and don't stay angry long, for mercy is your specialty. That's what you love most. And compassion is on its way to us. You'll stamp out our wrongdoing. You'll sink our sins to the bottom of the ocean. (Micah 7:18-19, MSG)

It would've been great if our camp were on the ocean. It's not, but it is on a lake. So you can imagine what we did with our rotten fruit. We each picked up a piece of rotten fruit, took that fruit out onto the deck and prayed—thanking God for his mercy and asking God to forgive our sins. Next came the very best part. We took our rotten fruit and threw it—as far and as hard as we could—into the depths of the lake.

Your rotten fruit isn't something you need to carry around in your back pocket so you can remind yourself of all the ways you mess up. It's something you toss as far and as hard as you can as you ask for God's forgiveness. (Your mom or dad might even let you toss some fruit on your own.) And as that fruit sinks into the depths of the sea (or the lake, the pond, or the river), we're freed to live a new life with Christ.

That's when we get to experience the good fruit from life with God. The Bible gives us a list of good fruit—maybe you've heard it before. The list includes love, joy, peace, patience, kindness, goodness, gentleness, and self-control (you can read the list in Galatians 5:22-23). These kinds of fruit show up when we have the Spirit of God in us. From time to time bad fruit will still pop up. But we just take that rotten fruit and toss it again. It sinks to the bottom of the sea and is gone. No more shame. No more gross, rotten fruit. Just grace. It's as simple—and amazing—as that.

13

Mile Marker Thirteen:
BECOMING YOU

"Therefore I intend always to remind you of these qualities, though you know them and are established in the truth that you have. I think it right, as long as I am in this body, to stir you up by way of reminder." (2 Peter 1:12-13, ESV)

"You will do well to pay attention as to a light shining in a dark place, until the day dawns and the morning star rises in your hearts." (2 Peter 1:19, ESV)

These two verses sum up what this whole book is about—and no, that doesn't mean you could've read just this chapter and gotten the whole point. But those four questions every girl asks—the questions we began this book with—are answered, or at least stirred up, in these two verses:

- Who am I?
- What do I want most in my life?
- What should I do?
- Who do I want to be?

Who Am I?

You experience a lot of uphills and downhills in who you are right now. You have hard issues like hiccups in confidence, losing your voice, self-consciousness, and puberty. And then you have really exciting changes like freedom, thirst, independence, and puberty. (Remember, puberty is an uphill-downhill-uphill-downhill kind of thing.)

You have days where you feel on top of the world—you love your friends, are getting along with your family, and are doing pretty well in school. And the next morning you wake up and have a rotten-fruit kind of day. Someone you thought was your friend spreads a rumor about you at school. You get in the car, and rather than crying to your mom like you really want to, you yell at her for being 10 minutes late. Up and down. Up and down. All of these emotions—and all of these days—are a part of who you are, or at least part of who you're becoming.

But you're more than that, too. You feel things more deeply than you ever have before. You care about your friends more. You want to know and understand truth. Who you are is stirring inside of you and starting to come together in solid form.

You can feel it. You say something to a friend and make a difference to her—and not only can you see it in her eyes, but you also know it somewhere way down inside of you. Some things bring you to life—music, art, or sports—experiences that awaken talents and bring you confidence you're just beginning to discover. You believe in some ideas you want to stand up for and speak out on, even when you feel self-conscious. Those are all significant parts of who you are.

You know these things much better than we do. The truth of who God made you to be is beginning to be established in you, as 2 Peter says. We just get to remind you.

What Do I Want Most in My Life?

God made you to want relationships—with friends, with family, with boys (at least someday), and with him. You want relationships to remind you of who you are and what you were made for. And so much of what you were made for was to love and be loved. God made you with the deep desire to connect.

The relationships that *stir you up by way of reminder* will mean the most to you. That means people will come into your life who make you want to be more of who you are. You won't really know how or why, but you'll act differently around them. You'll want to be kinder and know God better just because you know those people. Those people stir you to be the person God made you to be. They will speak to those deeper parts of who you are and draw them out. They'll encourage you and challenge you. They'll love you for who you are and at the same time make you want to be even better.

Find those relationships. Put yourself in places where you'll be stirred—and stir others, too. Just as God made you want to be loved, God also made you want to love. You'll feel more confidence and joy in who God made you to be as you help someone else discover the same thing.

What Should I Do?

Pay attention to the darkness—and the light. The darkness comes in many forms—it can come from the Internet, peer pressure, drugs, alcohol, body image, and a whole lot of other struggles that will surround you as you walk through these next several years of life. You'll have dark times. Maybe you'll be drawn to that darkness, and your friends will get tangled up with it. If that happens, remember the darkness isn't what you want. It will not bring you joy, confidence, or peace of any kind. Darkness just leads to deeper darkness.

Isaiah 9:2 says, "The people walking in darkness have seen a great light; on those living in the land of deep darkness a light has dawned." Jesus is that light. He takes our rotten fruit and throws it into the depths of the sea. God forgives us. He loves and delights in us and calls us away from the darkness and into the light. Pay attention to that light—the light of Christ and the light God placed inside you.

Who Do I Want to Be?

A poem in one of our favorite movies, *Akeelah and the Bee*, speaks to the girls we know, girls like you. Like the verses in 2 Peter, the poem has a lot to do with who we believe girls want to be:

> Our deepest fear is not that we are inadequate.
> Our deepest fear is that we are powerful
> beyond measure.
> It is our light, not our darkness that most
> frightens us.
> We ask ourselves—who am I to be brilliant,
> gorgeous, talented, fabulous?
> Actually, who are we not to be?

And we like this quote, too:

> You are a child of God. Your playing small does not serve the world. There is nothing enlightened about shrinking so that other people do not feel insecure around you. We were born to manifest the glory of God that is within us. It is not just in some of us, it is in everyone. And as we let our light shine, we unconsciously give other people permission to do the same. As we are liberated from our own fears, our presence automatically liberates others. (Williamson, 190-191)

If you're honest, you really want to be brilliant, gorgeous, talented, and fabulous. We all do. But it can be much scarier to be those things than to sit in a dark corner. Why? Because to be all those things means you have to have a voice. It means you have to let go of all the things like self-consciousness and rotten fruit that hold you back.

Whether you feel like it or not, you have God's light shining inside of you. God made you to be a light to the world. The verse in 2 Peter ends with the phrase "until the day dawns and the morning star rises in your hearts." That means until Jesus comes back, we are to be light—God's light—to each other. We're to stir and love and remind each other of who God is and who God made us to be. Your light is unlike anyone else's has been or ever will be. You are different. Unique. God made you to shine, to have a voice, to be you.

My (Sissy's) grandmother's highest compliment she ever paid was that something was "becoming." When she said a shirt was becoming on me, she meant it was beautiful. And you are beautiful. You're *becoming* because God placed beauty deep inside you—beauty that pours out of who you are.

Although the uphills will be tough in the years between 11 and 14, we don't want you to grow weary or lose heart. Keep running—or pedaling. God is developing strength inside of you. God has placed joy before you. God is growing depth and creativity and kindness and compassion and so much good that will be a part of you for the rest of your life. You're becoming. And on this road you will fall and fail, get back up, and fall again. But as you fix your eyes on Jesus, you can keep pedaling. Together the mirrors and maps will point you toward God and toward the brilliant, gorgeous, talented, fabulous, unique person he made you to be.

Therefore, since we are surrounded by such a great cloud of witnesses, let us throw off everything that hinders and the sin that so easily entangles. And let us run with perseverance the race marked out for us, fixing our eyes on Jesus, the pioneer and perfecter of faith. For the joy set before him he endured the cross, scorning its shame, and sat down at the right hand of the throne of God. Consider him who endured such opposition from sinners, so that you will not grow weary and lose heart. (Hebrews 12:1-3)

Works Cited

Gurian, Michael, *The Wonder of Girls* (New York: Pocket Books, 2002).

Montgomery, Lucy Maud, *Anne of Green Gables* (Philadelphia: Courage Books, 1993.

Williamson, Marianne, *A Return to Love: Reflections on the Principles of a Course in Miracles* (New York: Harper Collins, 1992).

If you've ever felt lonely, abandoned, lost, or unloved, you're not alone. Although she's a successful Gotee recording artist today, Stephanie Smith has had her fair share of hurt and heartbreak. Growing up fatherless, she struggled with her identity, self-esteem, and so much more. But today, she's found hope in God that she believes can help you through your own heartaches and brokenness.

Crossroads
The Teenage Girl's Guide to Emotional Wounds
Stephanie Smith
RETAIL $9.99
ISBN 978-0-310-28550-2

Visit www.invertbooks.com or your local bookstore.

Everyone has secrets, but you don't have to live with your pain all alone. *Secret Survivors* tells the compelling, true stories of people who have lived through painful secrets. As you read stories about rape, addiction, cutting, abuse, abortion, and more, you'll find the strength to share your own story and start healing, and you may even discover how to help a friend in pain.

Secret Survivors
Real-Life Stories to Give You Hope for Healing
Jen Howver & Megan Hutchinson
RETAIL $12.99
ISBN 978-0-310-28322-5

If you don't understand why you feel, act, or think the way you do now, and life used to be so simple, you're not alone—you're growing up! Listen to other girls like you, and two women who know a lot about what you're going through. You'll start to understand who you are and you'll see the wonderful person you're becoming.

Growing Up Without Getting Lost
Discovering Your Identity in Christ
Melissa Trevathan & Sissy Goff
RETAIL $16.99
ISBN 978-0-310-27917-4

Brooklyn Lindsey grew up dreaming of being a supermodel. But it wasn't until she became a youth pastor that she realized God had plans for her to be a different kind of "supermodel."

God has a plan for you, too—and it's probably bigger than anything you could ever imagine. In this book you'll begin to reshape the way you see yourself and the way you dream.

Confessions of a Not-So-Supermodel
Faith, Friends, and Festival Queens
Brooklyn Lindsey
RETAIL $9.99
ISBN 978-0-310-27753-8

It's hard to know who the real Jesus is when so many people are trying to prove him as a fake or a fraud. Some people believe he never rose from the dead, or that you can't trust the Bible because humans have made changes to the text. A former atheist and journalist has done extensive research to uncover the real Jesus, and he's bringing you his findings so you can discover the truth for yourself.

The Case for the Real Jesus
A Journalist Investigates Current Challenges to Christianity
Lee Strobel with Jane Vogel
RETAIL $9.99
ISBN 978-0-310-28323-2